VALUABLE CHANGE
WHAT YOU NEED TO KNOW TO ENSURE YOUR CHANGE PAYS OFF

Brendon Baker

COPYRIGHT © 2021
VALUABLE CHANGE CO.

All rights reserved.

First Published 2021
Hardcover ISBN: 978-0-6451227-0-1
Paperback ISBN: 978-0-6451227-1-8
eBook ISBN: 78-0-6451227-2-5

CONTENTS

A Quick Note from the Author vi

Introduction

About Valuable Change 2
Some Scary Stats and Worthless Projects 2
What You Are Going to Get From This Book 5

Part One: Your Change

Chapter 1: Ask the Right Questions 12
The Essence of a Valuable Project 12
Don't Fall into The Money Trap 13
Learning from Failure 16
Valuable Question One: Why Are We Doing It? 18
Valuable Question Two: How Will We Prove It? 25
Valuable Question Three: What Are We Doing? 33
The Top Four Mistakes Projects Make 38

Chapter 2: Have A Spine 41
The Secret to Building Valuable Projects 41
Two Steps, That's It. 43
Build the Core 47
SO WHAT – Creating Your VQM 56
PROOF – How You Plan to Show Off 66
HOW – Answering the *'Delivery 6'* 68

Chapter 3: Drive the Core 72

The Impossible Victory 72
The Power of A Better Platform 78
Driver Aid 1: Valuable Decisions 81
Driver Aid 2: The Learning Habit 91
Driver Aid 3: Simplest Practical Artefacts (SPAs) 108
The Truth About Driver's Aids 118

Part Two: Your People

Chapter 4: Stack The Value Equation 120

Why We Do Things (Or Don't) 120
The Interesting Science Behind It 123
Stacking the Equation in Your Favour: A Sustainable Reward 126
Stacking the Equation in Your Favour: The PITA Factor 134
Deploying The Value Equation In Your Change 143
Gamification: The Art of Creating New Rewards 145
A Final Note On A Valuable Mindset 154

Chapter 5: Rally Your People 155

The Better, More Effective Way: The VP Approach 157
Build and Protect Core Momentum: Elevating from Despair to Fanaticism . 161
Identifying Where You (and Your Team) Are 165
Strategies To Level Up 166
Maintaining High Momentum 186

Chapter 6: Forge Influential Champions & Communities 187

Identify and Enlist Internal Influencers: Find the Right People in Your Organisation to Recruit to Your Cause 188
Engage & Grow through Community: The Essence of A Great Community 206
But Wait There's More! Bonus Tactic: How To Truly Shift Capability 212
Rallying is Hard Work 219

Chapter 7: Value Balance Your Change Support 220

The Secret Behind Effective Change Support 222
Why Command & Control Isn't The Answer 223
An Imbalanced Equation 229
Breaking The Cycle 230
The Path To The High Value Service Cycle 232
A Final Note on Change Support 236

Part Three: Your Next Move

Chapter 8: Shift To Valuable Change 238

Ripple Area 1: Your Change Core 243
Ripple Area 2: Inside Your Change 244
Ripple Area 3: Outside Your Change 244
Valuable Change is a Journey not a Destination 246

Chapter 9: TL;DR: Valuable Change In A Nutshell 247

About Valuable Change 248
Your Change 249
Your People 251
Your Next Move – Shift To Valuable Change 257

Acknowedgements

Acknowledgements 260
About The Author: Brendon Baker 262

VALUABLE CHANGE

A Quick Note from the Author

My personal philosophy is that a book is worth reading if it gives you at least one usable good idea. A book is twice as valuable if you have an 'ah-ha' moment, where you and the content have this wonderful click. After all, as Mr. Million Dollar Consultant, Alan Weiss says:

> *"If you improve by just 1% every day, you will be twice as good in just 70 days".*

I consider my job done here if there's at least one thing in the next 270 or so pages that makes you sit back, look out the window and say:

> *"Hmm... I like that. I might just try it".*

The challenge I have is that I don't know what piece of content is going to create that moment for you. And to make it more difficult - that moment is going to be different for each reader.

So, I am left with just one choice – to fill this book with a tonne of good, practical ideas and strategies that I've found work time and time again. Then, no matter what it is you decide to pick up from this book, I'll rest well at night knowing that it'll work and more importantly - it'll make your life better.

We are all involved in changing our organisations, whether we know it or not. This book will help anyone who reads it better drive real value out of that change.

But there's a quick word of warning here. Everything you are about to read is unusually logical. There is a trap that comes with stripping things down to the point of logical simplicity – and that is you may be tempted to consider it as self-evident and treat it as such.

Don't.

As I will echo throughout this book. Simplicity is not simpleness. We all have a habit of overcomplicating things. Remember Occam's Razor - the simplest explanation is usually the right one.

See you inside.

BB

INTRODUCTION

About Valuable Change

Some Scary Stats and Worthless Projects

Can I share with you a secret?

...I warn you, it's a daunting one.

OK, here it is. Across the $10 Billion in change that I've consulted on, only 15% have been able to succinctly answer these three simple, but wholly fundamental questions:

1) Why are we changing?
2) How will we know when we are successful? (and prove it)
3) What are we doing?

So yes, that means 85% of these projects are venturing in the dark. Throwing money at an unknown result. This isn't just accepting ambiguity; this is driving off a cliff, blindfolded and hoping the car flies. And it gets worse...

I'm going to take some liberty here and assume that you're a reasonable person.

So, reader, as a reasonable person, if you were leading a change project across your organisation (and you may well be already), *when* would you expect to be able to answer the above three questions about your change?

If you answered anything earlier than the back half of the project, then you are doing better than 95% of that $10 Billion. Congratulations, you are in that desirable 5%!

But let me ask you – does your reality match this? Can your projects answer these questions clearly and succinctly? And if they do, are decisions being made with this information front of mind?

'*..But Brendon',* you may say, '*We've tried formalising this type of thing in the past and all we did was create red tape. Our teams are good at delivering. We prefer to just let them get on with it."*

And to this I say, I hear you. I truly do. I've been there, and I agree.

However, do you find you have projects that never end?

Or, perhaps you have projects that experience endless requests for change?

What about projects that everyone *'just sort of knows'* what the scope is, but if I asked everyone to list it, I would get 50 different answers?

Or perhaps you are experiencing the worst of it; a project that delivers something that doesn't solve the original problem. **A worthless project.**

If so, then maybe it is time to look at a better way. The good news is that you can have your cake and eat it. After all, I wouldn't be writing this book if I didn't have a streamlined and practical way to help you create more valuable projects.

What You Are Going to Get From This Book

This book will provide you with what you need to set the best possible course for your projects. It will show you how you can drive truly valuable change within your organisation. You will soon be ramping up the return on your projects, turning outcomes into reality, generating untold momentum, and eliminating fluffy paper claims. When you are running valuable change projects, you can say goodbye to: slow project start-ups, unwieldy plans, teams stuck in despair, communities and training that just doesn't work, and the endless teams of graduates sitting in dark rooms staring at spreadsheets[1].

Here's the thing, if all you needed was a good model then you would have done it already.

Valuable Change is more than a model. There are other books and guides whose entire premise is walking you through their new fandangled model. However, I prefer a different approach.

Here we aren't just focused on creating valuable projects - but ensuring your future projects *stay* valuable. What this means is that along with the right questions to ask, this book also gives you the secret to making it work, key techniques to accelerate your change, and the basis for shifting to value within your own organisation.

Accordingly, this book is structured into three parts.

---

[1] Much to the relief of both you and the graduate, I'm sure.

Part One: Your Change sets you up for success by sharing the core architecture of a valuable project. You will get the model that works time and time again. I have put this upfront on purpose. I strongly believe that we should only be delivering valuable projects, so I am giving you both the core and the mechanics of what Valuable Change looks like as soon as I possibly can.

Part One is broken into three chapters:

> In Chapter One, **Ask the Right Questions**, you will learn the essence of what makes a project valuable. We walk through the three core Valuable Questions each change initiative must answer, and I'll share crucial techniques to enable you to rapidly get to the heart of your project. You will learn why it's not all about profit or cost savings, but rather why clarity and delivery of purpose is more important when evaluating a project.[2]. Chapter one also gives you the top four fatal mistakes that are destroying most projects' chances of creating Value.
>
> In Chapter Two, **Have A Spine**, I give you the model that I use time and time again to drive Valuable Change. This model, which forms your project's spine, has a track record of providing you with early and regular visibility of a project's feasibility while simultaneously making the lives of your project team(s) easier. You will finally be structuring and connecting the right information and decisions at the right time. This saves huge amounts of

---

[2] Something that is particularly important to keep in mind in the Government and Not-For-Profit sectors.

time and effort (and last-minute thinking!). It can't be overstated how much a strong Valuable Change spine increases the efficiencies of your projects while reducing the average time that it takes your organisation to have a project up and running.

In Chapter Three, **Drive The Core**, I share with you what the auto racing industry knows, which we are all ignoring – the secret to consistent success! You will learn how to build the right platform to keep value front of mind in your change as it progresses from idea to reality. Not only does this keep your projects on rails, but it sets them up to accelerate the translation of those initial paper claims into reality.

Unfortunately, there is very little in this book you can do alone. Which is why, **Part Two: Your People**, provides you with the tools to rally the momentum and support needed to create truly Valuable Change.

Part Two is broken into four Chapters:

In Chapter Four, **Stack The Value Equation**, drawing from modern behavioural science, you will uncover the equation that underpins our decisions on whether or not to do something. This is crucial knowledge when you're driving Valuable Change through your organisation. Through this chapter you will learn the art of stacking the equation in your favour by maximising reward and minimising pain. I'll then share with you one amazing way to create new rewards out of thin air.

Chapter Five is **Rally Your People**. Simply put - your teams will make or break your efforts to deliver Valuable Change. No longer can they be cogs in the engine – you need active involvement and embedded innovation. In Chapter Five we walk through each of the five levels of project team momentum, and the strategies that you will use to generate real change fanaticism - no matter your project's current morale.

Chapter Six, **Forge Influential Champions & Communities** turns our focus outward to the rest of your organisation and stakeholder base. This chapter contains the two most powerful shortcuts to generating change buy-in that I've ever seen. First you will learn how to leverage cutting edge insights from the field of network science to find and identify the most influential people in your organisation. Can you imagine the power your change could wield with those people on your side? Well, I've got great news for you – it's possible. And it doesn't take complex analysis or a degree in data science... In fact, it will only take you two questions to find them. We then shift gears and explore the second shortcut to generating insane levels of buy-in: Communities. Yes, I admit that communities are a recent '*flavour of the month*', and most end up failing... But they're a flavour of the month for a reason. When done right, a community is an insanely powerful tool for our change initiatives. In this chapter you will learn the secret to both preventing community failure and ensuring ongoing prosperity. Finally, I throw in a bonus technique for you here – how to design training programs that actually pay off.

The final chapter in Part 2 is Chapter Seven, **_Value Balance Your Change Support_**. Your Change Support Function is often the conduit between your change efforts and your organisation's bureaucratic friction. Whether it's reporting, governance, audits, forecasting, risk profiling, investment analysis or one of the other 50+ things a change support function can do. But there's a major problem most organisations face here. Most change support functions become burdensome overheads. Thankfully not all change support functions operate this way. The truly successful ones operate with a different mindset. One of service. In this chapter you will learn both why that's the case, and how to ensure your change is supported using mechanisms built on high value and high trust.

Part Three: Your Next Move is where we will bring it all together. Part Three is broken into two Chapters:

In Chapter Eight, **_Shift To Valuable Change_**, it's time to turn what's in these pages into your new reality. You will be shown how all the pieces of the puzzle that we explored through Parts One and Two of this book fit together. Further, you will learn why you must channel your inner Bruce Lee and think like a body of water when doing so.

Chapter Nine, **_TL;DR: Valuable Change In A Nutshell_**, is unfortunately not what a squirrel needs to know about creating valuable organisational change, but rather is this book in summary. It's perfect for those that are time poor or just want the 'Cliffs Notes' version. This chapter draws from the internet-concept of *TL;DR*, or *'Too Long; Didn't Read'*. A concept that started as a cheeky response to something that was too long to bother reading. It slowly evolved into a voluntary shorthand at the end of longer pieces of internet commentary that offered a summary of the text that came before it. So Chapter Nine is this book's *'TL;DR',* where I cram as many of the key concepts and takeaways from the previous 260 odd pages into just 10. It's for those that want to get a sense of this book in a nutshell, or for those who have read the book and just need a quick reminder. However, this chapter comes with a warning - it is content packed but doesn't hold the broader context and nuance that comes from reading the rest of this book.

Also, just a little housekeeping before we dive in. Please note that throughout this book I'll be using the terms '*Project*', '*Program*' and '*Initiative*' interchangeably to represent a concerted effort to change something whether internal or external to your organisation.

Still with me? Great. Let's do it.

PART ONE: YOUR CHANGE

Chapter 1: Ask the Right Questions

The Essence of a Valuable Project

OK, let's get straight to the heart of the matter. What makes a change valuable?

In short – **A Valuable Change is one that solves a key organisational need or desire.** It's truly as simple as that.

The trick is ensuring that your change actually solves that need or desire, and this is where the art of asking the right questions becomes your key tool. A concise and considered answer to all three Valuable Questions is crucial for creating a great return on your project investment.

Don't Fall into The Money Trap

But first... I want you to close your eyes with me for a moment and imagine yourself sitting outside the board room of one of the largest retail chains in Australia. Maybe you're nervous, sitting there fidgeting with your pen. Or perhaps you're a slick operator, sitting in a calm silence. Either way, you know this is not going to be a fun meeting. You are about to break some devastating news to the CEO and Owner. To make it worse, this is a man not known for his patience or good nature.

You are about to inform him that the half a billion-dollar portfolio of projects that you've been asked to audit is on track to deliver only 50% of its expected financial return...

Finally, the door opens, and your name is called. You walk in and greet the room.

As a seasoned professional, you warm the room up with some good humour and your positive findings.

> *"The projects are delivering well. Systems and processes are, on the whole, on track."*

...Then you break the news.

> *"The expected financial benefits across the portfolio were over estimated. By a factor of 2 to 1."*

There is silence... An awkward stillness fills the room. Then your intuition detects something. Your brain switches to slow-motion as you hear a noise... a 'whooshing' noise, that seems to be getting louder. Then you start to see it out of the corner of your eye... a shiny object comes hurtling at your head.

What do you do?

Tell me, would your first reaction be to duck? Because if so, then you may well have been as lucky as a friend of mine was in this exact situation. He too managed to dodge the glass jug that was thrown at him by this short-tempered CEO. My friend's quick reactions saved him from a potentially large hospital stay, reducing the damage to just a broken water jug and a cracked window.

This is a story of a CEO who deeply understands that every change initiative is an investment. The feeling was particularly acute for this man as it was his personal wealth that was invested with the organisation. Where this CEO missed the mark, well aside from the physical violence, was that he got so caught up in the financial return.

And this is how we arrive at the first common misconception we challenge in this book: As each change initiative is an investment, many leaders get caught in the trap of always expecting a money-based return.

The reality is that value doesn't always come in the form of tangible cost savings or increased revenue. Sometimes an organisation wants to shift its culture, or stop using an IT system that people don't like, or improve its customer experience, or make some other shift to set itself up for the future. There are also times when an organisation isn't focused internally – perhaps it's investing for the betterment of a vulnerable community or other philanthropic goal. The key to all these elements is that a project needs to be solving an organisational need or desire. The art here is in figuring out what it's going to do to solve it, and how it's going to prove it has done so.

> ### A COMMON TRAP
> A common trap that Government and Not-For-Profit (NFP) organisations fall into is requiring their projects to have a financial return. These organisations often get caught up in purely mathematical exercises to demonstrate the millions of different ways that the Government or NFP will be more efficient after the project delivers its work.
>
> Interestingly, the polar opposite of this trap is also equally found through Government and NFP organisations – the dangerous thinking that *"We aren't profit-driven, so we don't need to prove we invested the money well"*.
>
> Neither of these are useful positions.

LEARNING FROM FAILURE

My key aim in this chapter is to illustrate the power of asking and then answering the right questions. What better way to do that than to look at what happens when the right questions are ignored? There are a multitude of examples we could draw on for that, but to really illustrate it, I've found us an elephant of a project.

In 2006 the Australian New South Wales (NSW) State Government Department of Education started one of its largest undertakings ever – the Learning Management and Business Reform project (known more widely as LMBR). The LMBR project was inherently ambitious in nature. It aimed to replace a 15-year old cluster of expensive and no longer suitable backend and learning management systems across the Department itself, 2230 public schools and its vocational TAFE[3] sites. The expected total cost for the project was $483 Million. Expected total time: 8 years.

The project progressed well for its first few years, delivering some early wins all within expectations. All seemed OK from the outside looking in.

It wasn't until late 2014, as the project was nearing its expected end date, that a bombshell dropped. It was revealed that the project was overspent and not even close to done. In fact, delving deeper, after the preceding years and circa $530 Million, the Department had only partially delivered its solution to 229 of the

---

[3] TAFE stands for Technical and Further Education. TAFE NSW is Australia's largest vocational education and training provider.

2230 schools. Just 10% of its target result at an already notable cost overrun. Unfortunately, even luck was not on the project's side, with public outcries by the Public Service Association (the workers' union) to halt the rollout – citing major system flaws and huge additional workloads for the staff at those 229 schools that had received the new system.

If we ratchet forward a further four years to 2018, with continued time and cost slippage, and more public embarrassment on the way (including misplacing $525M in TAFE revenue in 2016); we arrive at the end of the LMBR journey. The final result: a 12-year project (50% longer than the original time estimate), and $755 Million in spend (+56% more than originally planned).

While there isn't direct audit data available for 2018, the key findings in the 2014 audit were that: "*The Department* [had] *yet to demonstrate that it* [would] *achieve* [any] *expected benefits*" [4].

If we temporarily put aside the fact that this project likely made some consulting partners very wealthy[5], LMBR is a great example of what happens when a project doesn't answer and link the three key Questions that underpin a Valuable Change. So, like a forensic analyst, let's delve deeper. Let's conduct a procedural autopsy of their failures to give us useful insight into why each of the Valuable Questions truly create Valuable Change.

---

[4] New South Wales Auditor-General's Report - Performance Audit - The Learning Management and Business Reform Program - Department of Education and Communities
[5] In 2014, 60% of that $530 Million was spent on contractors and consultants.

VALUABLE QUESTION ONE: WHY ARE WE DOING IT?

> *"Very few people or companies can clearly articulate WHY they do what they do. ...People don't buy WHAT you do, they buy WHY you do it."*
>
> *- Simon Sinek*

In the quote above, Simon clicks into why the first Valuable Question is *"Why Are We Doing It?"*. In short – there are two reasons it's absolutely crucial to answer this question clearly as early as we possibly can.

1) First is that, unless you're on the bleeding edge of 'cool tech', no one is motivated by what you're doing. And, even if you are on the bleeding edge, not everyone is motivated by future tech. It's the **WHY** you're doing it that drives engagement. Get this right and you will find that winning stakeholder buy-in becomes dramatically easier. Seriously, we are talking a night and day level of difference here. Whether this is in trying to convince investment boards to allocate you funding, or explaining why your new restructure is a good idea for the 650 staff affected – a clear WHY makes your life easier.

2) The second amazing thing that happens when you answer this Valuable Question is that you automatically start to build in regular checks on the project's viability. By this I mean, you start asking the logical follow-up question – *"Does this project **still** make sense?"*. It's this one-two punch combination of questions that will have one of the

largest impacts on driving up your project return on investment while simultaneously cutting down your project lengths.

GETTING TO YOUR PROJECT'S WHY

Unfortunately, our elephant – the LMBR Project - failed to capitalise on either of the awesome advantages of answering the project 'WHY'. Let's explore.

Let's first look at the LMBR's formal stated project 'WHY'.

> The department stated that *'the reasons for proceeding with the LMBR program were that the existing finance, human resources, payroll and student administration systems were over 15 years old, technically obsolete, complex, costly to maintain, and did not meet the Department's business requirements.'*

Anyone excited yet? No? Hmm... Maybe if we go on it'll get a little better:

> *'There were over 100 applications being used by schools and TAFEs to* [supplement the existing systems' deficiencies]. *This meant there was duplication of effort and inefficient and inconsistent manual processes across the Department. The LMBR program was designed to address these issues.'*

Can you hear a strong enough call for a $750 Million spend and 12 years of effort in any of the above? Because I can't. It seems that LMBR had a clarity of 'WHY' problem. Simply put – having an old system is not a good enough WHY for any project. But maybe I'm being a little harsh.

Let's have a look at the outcomes they were expecting... (note they were quite lengthy, so I've abbreviated them for both our sanity).

1. *Improve the range of system delivery channels*
2. *Improve service delivery to parents, students, staff and businesses*
3. *Deliver efficiencies by reallocating back-office to frontline*
4. *Improve access to services from any internet anywhere in the world*
5. *Introduce new standardised processes across the department*
6. *Improve data integrity and consistency of employee information*

...and so on, and so on. It keeps going.

How about now? Excited?

Hmm... me neither. Perhaps it's time to share one of the most important techniques you will learn in this book. It's just two words, yet they will give you borderline super-powers.

Are you ready for them?

OK, here they are:

"So what?"

It's a simple, two word response that you can use again, and again, and again to drill down to the heart of your project's WHY.

Let's try it out – let's start at the beginning.

> "The reasons for proceeding with the LMBR program were that the existing finance, human resources, payroll and student administration systems were over 15 years old, technically obsolete, complex, costly to maintain, and did not meet the Department's business requirements.'

Now say it with me – **'So What?!'**.

It's 15 years old – so what? Why does that matter?

It's complex and costly to maintain – so what? You've been affording it all these years, what's changed?

It didn't meet the Department's business requirements – again, so what? Things still seem to get done don't' they?

What we all need to keep in mind here is that, outside of a small group of people close to your project – no one else cares about what you're doing unless you can provide a strong and clear WHY.

I'll say that again because it's so easy to miss.

Outside of a small group of people close to your project – **no one else cares** about what you're doing **unless you can provide a strong and clear WHY.**

Coming back to LMBR - in all honesty we could have said their entire two paragraphs in just a few words. Let me show you.

It's 15 years old – oh, so the systems are ancient and clunky, perhaps even a little embarrassing to sit in front of every day, when at home you use beautiful web-apps that are available for free.

It's complex and costly? Ah, so maybe it's a pain in the ass to use then?

It's not meeting the Department's business requirements? Hmm... so it's frustrating and only does a half-job?

And there we are. Using a little bit of *'so what'* magic we arrive at something that looks like this:

> '*The Department's current systems are old, clunky and frustrating to use.*' [6]

Now we're getting somewhere.

Let's look at a few more of the snippets they had.

> '*LMBR will Improve service delivery to parents, students, staff and business*'

So what? Are we making their lives easier? Or just better informed? Or are we wowing them with how 'tech-savvy' we are?

---

[6] And yes, we could and perhaps should '*so what*' this sentence too.

> '*LMBR will improve access to services from any internet anywhere in the world*'.

Now if I'm honest, this one isn't too bad. But once again – 'so what?'. What are we enabling here? Working from home? (this was well before COVID-19, so that's unlikely). Are we expecting teachers to write reports while on their overseas holidays? Or maybe we are making student results available to parents, no matter where they are in the world?

And we can continue on and on.

But for the sake of this example, let's make a few assumptions and see if we can bring this together. Here's our first attempt at a *'So What'* summary:

> '*We know that the Department's current systems are old, clunky and frustrating. Frankly, we're a little embarrassed of them too. So, we're changing things. Our aim is to make your everyday life a little easier.*
>
> *With your help, we're redefining the interactions between front end and back end, between teachers and parents, and between tutors and students. We're sick of you having to run 100 different systems in your school or TAFE just to get the results you're looking for. One system, accessible anywhere, with the information you need at your fingertips.*'

Too much? Maybe. But it's dramatically more exciting. Maybe not $750 Million exciting, but it is better.

Now you tell me, if we were then to apply our 'one-two punch' combo to this project by asking '*does this project still make sense?*' – could we have avoided the very situation that the real life LMBR project found itself in.

In 2014, across the pilot group of schools, a whopping 60% stated they had received no benefit at all!

Or even the ridiculous situation that the LMBR affected schools ended up in. They were hit with a new finance system that shifted them from cash-based to accrual accounting in October 2012. Guess when training on accrual accounting was available to the schools? ...May 2014. Almost 2 full years later.

Would this have happened in a project that had stated its WHY as

"Our aim is to make your everyday life a little easier."

and then kept that aim front of mind each and every decision?...

No. It wouldn't have.

This is the power of having a damn good answer to *"Why Are We Doing It?"*.

VALUABLE QUESTION TWO:
HOW WILL WE PROVE IT?

"What can be asserted without evidence can also be dismissed without evidence."

- Christopher Hitchens

And so we arrive at our second Valuable Question – "*How Will We Prove It?*". That is, how will we prove we've achieved our project WHY.

This question takes a stand against the loose, fluffy claims that we're all a little guilty of putting down on paper to justify what we want to do.

Perhaps you aren't sure what I mean?

I'm talking about those things that we have no intention of actually measuring. Here's a few examples, but in honesty, the list is endless.

After we complete our awesome project:

- *Staff will be more engaged.*
- *Our processes will be more effective, have greater efficiency and will have better engagement.*
- *Our systems will be more effective and efficient.*
- *Our users will have a better experience.*
- *Reporting lines will be clearer.*

And so on.

What we need to accept here is that the burden of proof for success lies with the project – even if success won't be known till long after the project closes.

I'll repeat that because it's the crux of this Valuable Question.

The burden of proof for success lies with the project – even if success won't be known till long after the project closes.

We need to figure out exactly what success looks like. This is known throughout the industry as 'Benefits Management'. The problem is that most of the industry over-complicates the hell out of it. I'm sure you too have seen the great armies of graduates working for the large consulting firms toiling away at purely mathematical exercises on why the next transformation program should go ahead. Or worse, great armies of graduates figuring out why the transformation program DID go ahead, explaining its purpose after the fact!

While I understand that sometimes measures of success aren't all that simple – if you can't communicate what your WHY is succinctly, you won't be able to communicate how you plan to demonstrate you have achieved your WHY.

Let's pick up where we left off with our hypothetical LMBR WHY from the second Valuable Question:

> *"Our aim is to make your everyday life a little easier."*

Now, I admit I have made my own life a little harder by choosing this as a WHY. It's venturing awfully close to being fluffy and unmeasurable, just like my earlier example dot points. The art for this one, or any of the previous points, is translating this into something that can be measured.

Let's break this down.

First, we need to figure out who the *'Your'* in this sentence is referring to. For the sake of this example, we are going to assume it's all staff that will use the new system.

Next let's look at the real crux of this WHY statement: *"everyday life a little easier"*. Here is where we would need to do some homework. There are two ways to make someone's life easier; either we solve frustrations, or we create new opportunities.

Given the context of this project – we are going to target their frustrations.

In real life you would likely run a workshop or three here to identify these areas but, as this is a hypothetical, we don't have that luxury. So, let's simplify things. Let's imagine we ran some workshops and we found that their top three frustrations were:

1) Staff would often have to sit, waiting for the system to process even the most basic transactions. In fact, it would often take up to 5 minutes for it to process even simple tasks.

2) The system would randomly crash. Initial indications are that is happening on average three times a week per user, losing the staffs' progress when it did.

3) The system wasn't user-friendly which meant that there were often mistakes made in working through more complex transactions, requiring the staff to have to re-do their work.

We now have some ways to make our staffs' lives easier.

In particular, we are targeting improvements in processing times, stability, and reducing the number of mistakes made due to user confusion. All we then need to do is set targets for these measures and shoot for them.

So, the answer to our second Valuable Question '*How Are We Going to Prove It?*' becomes:

"We are going to eliminate the top sources of staff frustrations and give them a more modern experience. This means processing times for simple transactions that are less than five seconds, a crash-free system (99% of the time) and a simpler, more satisfying user experience – proven by survey results across a cross-section of staff."

Unfortunately, the real life LMBR didn't get to this level of clarity. They got caught in the money-trap, requiring $Millions in imaginary cost savings. By imaginary I mean that their armies of graduates would come up with creative ways of trying to create value for the project. For example, saving several minutes per day of every staff member – when added up creates a nice big number.

A number that **isn't real.**

You can tell it's not real because not a single budget or forecast would, or should, be adjusted using it. In reality that staff member would probably just spend those minutes making an additional cup of tea!

This is what happens when you treat your responsibility to prove success as a 'tick and flick' exercise. When you forget your burden of proof responsibility you can list as many imaginary project benefits as you like. After all, if there's no need to prove it, then a nice long list of benefits makes your project look so much better. Valuable Changes don't exist in our imaginations. They focus on reality. A Valuable Project backs its WHY with action. It creates the tactical plans on how to prove it has achieved its WHY.

A Tale of Two Projects

The Australian Taxation Office (ATO) asked me to help them answer the second Valuable Question for a portfolio of their IT projects. Across the portfolio there are two change initiatives that I want to show and tell briefly here as they give a good representation of how sometimes this question requires simple logic and other times a little lateral thinking.

The first was a straight shot through to goal.

One of the ATO's software vendors were looking to exit a product offering. This was a product that the ATO was using quite heavily to connect and integrate their systems. So, the vendor put into place a couple of new contractual stipulations:

> First, a license cap was set, which limited the number of licenses that the ATO could consume at current pricing.
>
> Second, the vendor gave 3-year advanced notice of a substantial upcoming price rise per license.

The ATO reacted as the vendor had hoped – it created a project in response. The project's WHY was simple:

> *"Heavily reduce the ATO's use of that application to avoid the cost increases".*

So how do you go about proving that?

This isn't a trick question. It truly was as simple as counting the number of licenses they had in use and were paying for. Then reducing that number.

Note that this is one of the times that converting this into real dollars makes sense. This was not imaginary money being pumped through a spreadsheet. Each ATO system that moved away from this expensive product meant a whole bunch of license cost savings in immediate cash.

So, this project's Valuable Questions 1 and 2 formed this:

"The license reduction project will heavily reduce the ATO's use of XYZ application. We are targeting a 50% reduction in license numbers, freeing up $1,000,000 [7] per year in planned license expenditure for use elsewhere in the department."

See, a straight shot.

Then we have the alternative. The curve ball[8].

The ATO were setting up a new gateway that focused on enabling better connections with both internal and external clients. The gateway would support small, fast connections that only dealt with relatively small amounts of data. The WHY was pretty simple:

"Enable clients to consume quick, small data services in real time".

But how do we prove that we've done it? The project WHY centred on enablement, so we needed to find ways to prove that it was enabling a better alternative. Through the Valuable Change toolset that you will see in Chapter 2, we drew out the following proofs:

1. The gateway will meet 'Gold level' industry standards for reliability and availability.
2. Users are happy to use the system, with an improved user experience as measured through surveys and uptake metrics.

---

[7] These numbers are generalised.
[8] Yes, I know I'm mixing sport metaphors here.

3. The time and effort to create a data connection via the new gateway would be much less than the existing systems.

This meant that their answers to Valuable Questions 1 and 2 became:

> *"The gateway project will enable clients to consume quick, small data services in real time. This means that our clients will enjoy Gold standard reliability, an improved user experience and a dramatically faster process for each and every new connection."*

Now that's something we can get behind.

A Valuable Project's Responsibility

If you take anything away from this section, please let it be this.

The onus for proof of success sits with the project.

This is one of the most powerful cultural shifts you can create in your change initiatives. This is the difference between a project that works in an imaginary world, and one that creates Real Value.

I know which I prefer.

VALUABLE QUESTION THREE: WHAT ARE WE DOING?

"Simplicity is the ultimate sophistication."

- Leonardo Di Vinci

Finally, we get to the third Valuable Question: *"What are we doing?"*.

Simple right?

You may be surprised at how many projects do not have enough clarity about what they are actually doing. I certainly was at first. What should be a no-brainer is often one of the thorns that ends up crippling projects down the line. Interestingly, I tend to find an inverse relationship between the amount of money spent on a project and the clarity and usefulness of its scoped inclusions, as I've shown below.

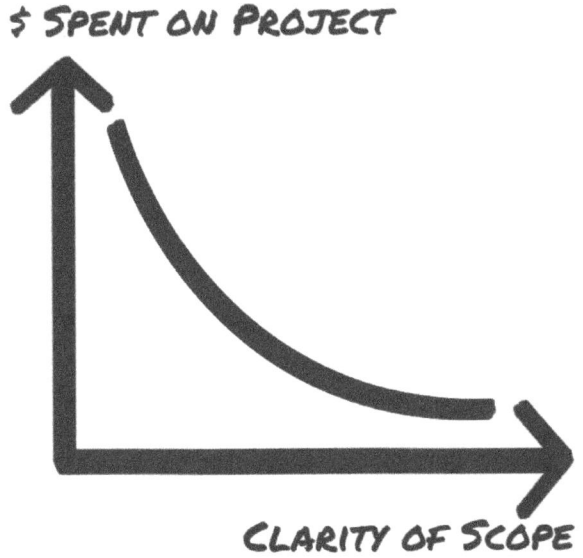

While I'll let you speculate in your own time why this relationship exists[9], what is more important is that we understand how a failure to properly define and agree early what the project is aiming to do can lead to dramatic damage later in a project's life.

Let's revisit the LMBR project. At $483 Million initial expected spend, based on the relationship we just discussed, we can reasonably expect that its clarity of scope was insufficiently considered.

And this certainly was the case.

Between 2006 and 2014 there were 7 attempts[10] at describing the project's scope, but only 2 of those were accepted and funded. Each of these 7 attempts had huge differences in what was considered 'in-scope' to be done. Further, a bunch of things that were initially meant to be completed in the project's first stage weren't delivered, despite being funded. This meant that the project had to double dip from the Department's funding pool to deliver what it had already promised.

It's probably then no surprise that this lack of clarity flowed through to the project's key recipients – that is, the 2230 schools and TAFE sites. Misconceptions, rumours, and unfulfilled promises seemed to be the norm for those on the receiving end of the LMBR rollout. In fact, of the schools surveyed in 2014, over 70% stated that installed components did not match what they were advised would be delivered.

---

[9] And I'm more than happy to speculate with you over a coffee one day
[10] 5 business cases and 2 scope redefinitions

You can then add in the fact that the project deployed systems that had known defects and required manual workarounds. This meant increased workloads for an already-stretched school staff. You can probably now see why the workers union was up in arms.

CLARITY OF WHAT YOU ARE DOING IS CRUCIAL

Now please don't misunderstand me - projects change, projects evolve, projects are living beasts.

But if we don't even attempt to clarify and ringfence what we are doing – and even more importantly, to hold ourselves to account for the delivery of these things – then how in the world do we expect to be successful?!

This is exactly why our third Valuable Question is '*What Are We Doing*?

Here's what an alternative situation looks like.

In 2015 the NSW State Archives were facing an interesting problem. Over 92% of their total archives were inaccessible. Not from a physical standpoint, but rather a contextual one. Simply put – there just wasn't enough data captured about what they had in storage to make it in any way findable or usable for themselves or members of the public. This was the inevitable result of being at the low-end of the budget food-chain while continuing to receive endless boxes of documents, cards and teddy bears[11] for conservation and storage. Nor was this a

---

[11] Yes, they also had to store teddy bears and other similar toys that had been left in memorial for the lives lost in the Lindt Café Siege that happened in Sydney in 2014.

problem unique to them. Most archives around the world find themselves facing a similar issue - industry benchmarks at the time averaged about 80% of total archives inaccessible.

So, the NSW Archives kicked off a project. They had managed to secure a cool one million dollars to throw at the problem. The catch – they only had 4 months to spend it, or they would lose it.

The goal was relatively simple: catalogue as many of the archives as they possibly could within that budget. Here is where most other projects would start getting lost in complexity. I mean, how would you tackle the millions of potential archives to target, many of which were completely unknown? We are literally talking about kilometres of unmarked boxes sitting on shelves in nuclear-safe storage.

And this is where the art of answering the right question came to strength. What this project did was nice and simple. First a target number was set. This was the number of archives that, if hit, would satisfy everyone's definition of *'Yes we've done well here'*. The final number chosen was based on the average number of archive items they catalogued in a year – 100,000.

The thing was - the project team didn't know which archives to tackle. There were a few known low-hanging fruit, a few pet projects, some sitting in conservation, plenty more turning up at their doors each month and a whole heap more sitting in boxes in dimly lit warehouses.

Without getting too deep into the solution – the project did something pretty clever. It established a flexible approach to the scope and focused on creating an ever-fed backlog of 'next up' items. It was one of the first projects to pioneer agile project management techniques for this type of work.

The end result of this was a creative, tangible solution to our third Valuable Question: *'What Are We Doing?'.*

The answer: *"Whatever is next in this backlog, achieving a minimum of 100,000 archive items".*

The power of this was immense. Each team knew exactly what they were up to, what was next and how they were contributing to this goal. Also, as their goal didn't have an upper limit, the project's only constraint was the amount of time and money left.

Any guesses on what the final number of archive items completed was, with that cool million and 4 months of concerted effort?

...Over 550,000! Five and a half times their initial target![12]

Not a bad result for an organisation with minimal project experience and unfavourable conditions. Maybe there is something to getting these Valuable Questions right...

---

[12] Which led to the project being nominated for a State Award. And in case you were wondering – yes, this is a project I led.

THE TOP FOUR MISTAKES PROJECTS MAKE

If you put this book down right now and just started injecting these 3 Valuable Questions into the heart of your projects, you would immediately see dramatic improvements in your ROIs, project speed, your stakeholder buy-in, your project status and more.

The clarity that these three questions provide for a change initiative is next to none.

However, there is power in learning from those who came before you. So here are the four most common mistakes that projects are making that are destroying their chance at creating value.

MISTAKE 1: MISREADING SIMPLICITY FOR SIMPLENESS

The first mistake that so many project leaders make is misreading simplicity for simpleness.

Yes, these questions are ridiculously simple. So simple that it's easy to under-estimate their importance. What this means is that many project leaders and teams ignore the effort to actually answer them. They run their projects on a loose assumption or 'common understanding' that everyone knows the answers to all 3 questions.

Please forgive my frankness here, but I'd bet that if I interviewed a cross section of these projects, I would get massive differences in understanding and clarity at the individual level. Achieving consistency and clarity is hard enough when these questions are answered! It becomes next to impossible if you run on a loose or assumed understanding.

In the next two chapters, we explore how and when to ask and answer the Valuable Questions to avoid loose assumptions and drive a strong and consistent WHY across your project.

MISTAKE 2: IT'S ONLY FOR THE BIG GUYS

The second most common mistake is assuming that these questions and this work is just for large projects and programs.

It's not.

It's for every project no matter the size. The impact and importance of these questions is the same.

The trick is to not overcook it.

MISTAKE 3: ANSWERING THE WHAT THEN FINDING THE WHY

Those that have been around projects for a little while may have noticed something about the order of these Valuable Questions. We didn't start with 'What are you doing', but rather we started with 'Why are you doing it'. This was conscious and on purpose. Starting with WHAT you are doing, rather than the WHY is one of the fastest ways to short circuit your project's Value. Yet despite this, I've seen this happen at every single client site I've worked with.

Pro tip – get the WHY clarified first. If you inherit a project and the WHAT is already somewhat known, it's important to take a moment, answer the WHY then re-ask whether the WHAT is actually the right solution.

Mistake 4: Trying To Do It Alone

Finally, it's crucial not to try to do this alone, or expect a sole team to run this for all your projects. It doesn't work. Truly Valuable Change needs to become a new culture within your projects. It must be embedded in each of your review and decision points.

VALUABLE CHANGE

Chapter 2: Have A Spine

The Secret to Building Valuable Projects

OK, it's time to give you the nuts and bolts of the model that underpins your journey to creating truly Valuable Change. But before I do, I want to prepare you. The Valuable Change model is deceiving in its simplicity...

>...But that's also the core of its power.

The model is the culmination of all the hard knocks, stupid mistakes, stunning success, late night celebrations, last minute rushes and various other sticking points from over $10 Billion in change initiatives. It's built on the principle of 'Simplicity First'. When pulling it together I have only kept what works and I've left the rest behind. I've stripped out the confusing jargon that is plaguing the industry and whittled it down to what is truly needed in your organisation.

The Valuable Change model is completely agnostic to what your project is and how you plan to deliver it. It doesn't care whether you're changing your light bulbs, redefining how you buy light bulbs, writing the policy on standardised light colouring or if you're building a system to give your customers full control of your office lighting.[13]

The model works. Full Stop.

You will have shorter project start up times.

You will better win, keep and allocate funding for your change programs.

You will reduce project document overhead – which in turn reduces your time and cost overhead.

You will slash unnecessary work from your project delivery – shrinking your project delivery timelines.

You will make value available from your projects faster – no matter whether you are delivering using a sequential (waterfall) or iterative (agile) delivery approach.

You will ensure that you're discussing the right things at the right times.

Your projects will make sense, and most importantly you will set them up to truly run.[14]

With all those in mind – here's my promise to you. I promise that the Valuable Change model will have a dramatic impact on your change initiatives. But, ONLY IF you embrace it into your project's core. It is not and should never be a tick and flick activity. There are many processes like that, but this isn't one of them. It's simple,

---

[13] And what a terrible idea that would be.
[14] *Cue chariots of fire theme*.

unbelievably lightweight and applies for any change you're undertaking.

So, if you are ready to grab it with both hands – let's do this.

Two Steps, That's It.

Anyone that has been around change long enough should be familiar with the typical project lifecycle. By that I mean:

Idea -› Setup/Plan -› Execute -› Close.

Each of these project stages have a multitude of other names they go by, but in general the flow of a project goes like this:

1) First, someone, somewhere, has an idea. Sometimes it's a good one. Sometimes it's a bad one. If it comes from the top, then most of the time it's going ahead – good or bad!

2) Then usually some more people look at the idea and it's thought through a little further. If it's a good enough idea, then they start up a project for it.

3) After a bare bones team is set up (often this is just a person or three), then one of two things happen.

    a. Either the team are given time to plan how to deliver,

    OR (and equally likely),

    b. The team are pressured to deliver straight away which leaves them tic-tacking between planning and delivering in parallel. We'd all like to claim this doesn't happen – but we all know that it does. For those that are delivering iteratively (those in the agile world), this blend of planning and delivering is claimed to be on purpose.

4) Through some mix of planning and delivering, the team gets it done. The project then closes down – either formally and on purpose, or without intention through attrition, decay and lost interest.

Any of that sound familiar? Great.

So, here's what Valuable projects do alongside that flow.

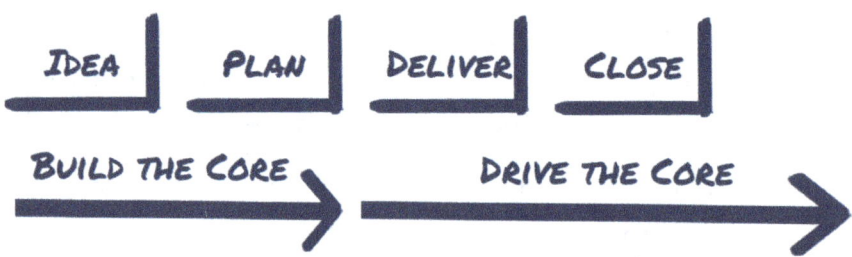

As you may have picked up already, I'm rather partial to simplicity, and here is no different. The Valuable Change model can be summarised in just 2 steps:

Step 1: Build the Core.

Step 2: Drive the Core.

In Step 1 you Build the Core of your project; creating what I call your project's spine. Similar to our own spines, your project's spine enables your projects to grow, communicate, and run.

When you get the spine right, you are connecting your change WHY with what it means for your organisation, how you plan to prove it and ultimately how you plan to achieve it. We will explore Step 1 later in this chapter.

Step 2 is to Drive the Core. You do this by building a fast, clear platform to deliver your change on. The platform should be regularly and continually improved to enable faster, clearer and more consistent results. Your platform must have your project's WHY and associated Proof Plan, (which we talk about soon), embedded into your everyday decision making. Further, your platform must ensure that your project is driven by its WHY, and not its WHAT. This means governance forums, planning work, key times and dates, team rituals, and delivery processes all need to be extensions from your project's core.

The impact of doing this cannot be overstated. Yet despite its power, the truth is that it's where most projects fall down. Some projects do have a solid go at defining their WHY... and then as soon as they win funding - they just shove it into a drawer and get about delivering.

To illustrate the point here, if we were to anthropomorphise our projects, let's consider what most would look like. First, I want you to bring into your mind an image of your favourite sports person.

Got one?

Great.

Now imagine them with no torso!

You should now be imagining a freakish abomination with their head and neck attached directly onto their pelvis.

Now I want you to add a truckload more muscle to just one of their legs – and then – swap the other leg out for an archetypical pirate peg-leg.

Are you suitably repulsed yet?

With these horrific transformations – would you still expect this athlete to continue to perform at a high standard? In 99% of cases the answer to that will be 'No way!'.

Yet this is what our projects look like.

We underdevelop our project torsos which are the key linkages between our project's WHY and WHAT. We then over-develop the delivery leg (the WHAT/HOW) and create an artificial view of how we will prove it (the PROOF). We then expect them to run a marathon (or in the case of an agile project – run sprints!).

It's a bit crazy really.

The good news – it doesn't have to be that way.

Build the Core

"Cannibals prefer those who have no spines."

- Stanislaw Lem

How good are your ideas?

By this I mean, besides a few black swan instances – how many times did you get it absolutely right the first time?

We all make assumptions that our 'gut instinct' is the right call for our projects, and that our intuitive reasoning is enough to set our projects up for success. But... what if it isn't?

Easily Swayed

In the 1970s the behavioural economists Daniel Kahneman and Amos Tversky ran a simple, but unusual experiment. Participants were given two simple tasks:

> First – spin a roulette wheel.
>
> Second – guess the percentage of the United Nations that were African.

To control the variables, Kahneman and Tversky had rigged the roulette wheel to restrict the possible landing spots to either the numbers 10 or 65.

Now, roulette has nothing to do with UN membership, and yet, that roulette spin had a dramatic impact on the participants answers.

Participants whose roulette wheel landed on 10, on average, guessed a 25% African UN membership. Those whose roulette wheel landed on 65, on average, guessed 45% membership. That's a 20% difference created just by first pre-conditioning participants' brains with meaningless data. This experiment illustrated the basis of a now well-known cognitive bias called anchoring. Anchoring is our tendency to depend too heavily on an initial piece of information to make subsequent judgements.

However, what's really scary is that the anchoring effect is just one of over 190 different cognitive biases that have now been uncovered. From optimism and choice-supporting bias to the Google and IKEA effects – making decisions is a cognitive minefield we traverse every day.

The basis for this is what Kahneman terms 'System 1' and 'System 2' thinking[15]. System 1, also known as 'Fast Thinking', underpins the vast majority of our decisions – it operates automatically and quickly, with little to no effort and no sense of voluntary control. Fast Thinking covers almost everything we do. Driving, eating, most of our conversations, how we move, and the vast majority of the rest of our lives. System 2, in contrast, is the slower, considered thinking process. It is the process of applying effort to our decisions and is often associated with the subjective experience of agency, choice, and concentration.

But what underpins a 'good' decision? And does this bias really matter?

---

[15] 'Thinking Fast and Slow', Daniel Kahneman

In an analysis[16] conducted by Carl Christian Rolf in 2005, human decision making was considered against several mathematical decision models. Carl compared decision making methods on six criteria:

- Transparency,
- Consistency,
- Accuracy,
- Improvement,
- Adaptability, and
- Speed.

The end result: Human decision-making beat mathematical decision models in just **one of the six** areas: **Speed**. Without a doubt this is due to our ability for 'System 1' fast thinking.

So, reader, is Speed enough to drive success in your organisation?

---

[16] 'Beyond Accuracy: How Models of Decision Making Compare to Human Decision Making', Carl Christian Rolf, 2005

Why Consider Why

Perhaps our human reliance on speed and 'effortless' decision making is why we, as change leaders, so often fall into the trap of moving straight from an idea to detailed planning (or worse, straight into execution). We forget to take a moment and check that the idea actually makes sense.

The problem here is that at some stage of the project we will connect the dots between what we are doing and why we are doing it. The key factors here are when that connection happens, and the corresponding cost of being wrong.

If you connect the dots before you do any work -> being wrong is as cheap as a few pieces of paper and a workshop or two.

However, if you connect the dots after you have delivered two entire phases of work -> being wrong can be catastrophic.

So that's what you will do in Step One: Build the Core. You will work through the logical linkages of the change, then play that back with those that have an active interest in the result of your change efforts. Countering both your System 1 'kneejerk' decisions and a few cognitive biases on the way[17]. Do this upfront and you will be amazed at the results you will see.

First, you will prevent time and money from being wasted on bad, illogical ideas. But what is ten times more powerful than that is you will be actively reducing your chances of getting stuck with one of the hardest decisions change leaders are faced with: whether or

---

[17] Confirmation, Optimism and IKEA biases to name a few.

not to accept sunk costs. This is a decision that is so hard that each year it keeps thousands of change initiatives alive simply because their leadership teams aren't willing to make the call to accept the loss.

Where possible – do ALL you can to avoid exposing yourself to a position where that decision needs to be made. Killing a failing project is far easier in theory than practice.

Second, getting your linkages clear upfront creates an opportunity for a ridiculously early pivot. In fact, this is one of the earliest and fastest ways of applying the agile management concept of 'failing fast'. The moment we have a logical disconnect between the WHAT and the WHY, we kill that WHAT element off.

This is powerful.

If you cut the scope of what you are doing before you even start, then your project becomes smaller, nimbler, and more importantly – targeted towards what will actually create the value for you. It helps you avoid falling prey to the Ego Trap[18] by helping you avoid adding project elements simply for your own personal vanity.

Third, upfront clarity dramatically boosts buy-in down the line. Ask anyone in the field of stakeholder management *'what is crucial for success?'* and you will hear the phrase *'engage early'*. Step One gives you the perfect way to create that engagement.

---

[18] We will explore the Ego Trap more in Chapter 4.

Introducing Your Project's Spine

If you have ever wondered what differentiates a superstar project from one that just spins its wheels in the mud – it is that project's spine. A project's spine dictates whether it will stand tall and weather the harsh winds of success, or whether it will be blown around – rolling down the road like a tumbleweed.

This is all about revealing the core of what you are trying to achieve. For best results, we are doing this during the typical Idea, Startup and Planning stages of a project. As we get more information, we strengthen and iteratively build the spine. In fact, many organisations simplify their start up processes by embracing and re-orienting around this project core. However, the great thing about this is that while we should endeavour to do the work upfront and early; every project, no matter how late in its life, can and will benefit by creating and strengthening its spine.

Like your own body, your project's spine is made up of a few key areas. Unlike our own spines though, a project's spine only has 4 key parts:

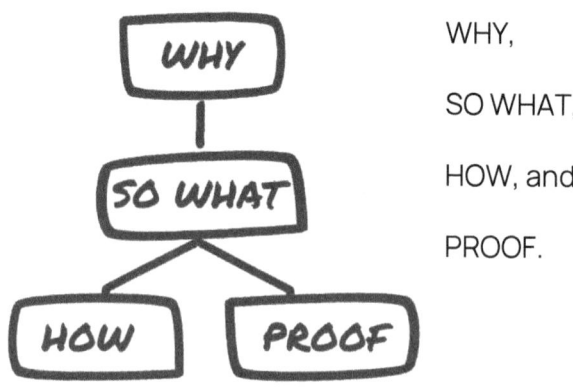

WHY,

SO WHAT,

HOW, and

PROOF.

You may also notice we shirk the standard, confusing terminology and jargon found throughout typical project practice. Less jargon means less confusion. Less confusion means higher adoption[19]. And that's a very good thing.

STARTING WITH WHY

As you may suspect, we start by answering the First Valuable Question (see Chapter 1): *'Why Are We Doing It?'*. This can take many forms, but in essence we are looking for a clear, inspiring statement of vision and intent. Be careful though, don't get caught up describing WHAT you are doing here. We don't want to accidentally create circular logic in our project spine. Rest assured that the WHAT will come later.

To help illustrate what I'm talking about here, I'll provide a few examples of good and not so good WHY statements. Note that while these may be simplistic, the *'how to improve'* commentary rings true across the majority of project WHYs I've encountered to date.

---

[19] We will explore other ways to maximise adoption in Part 2 of this book.

NOT SO GOOD	HOW TO IMPROVE	BETTER
The organisation has a need for a new database to capture our client payment data.	*We are stuck describing the WHAT.* *WHY does the organisation need a new database?*	We receive over $1B in client fees each year. However, it's estimated that 10% of that yearly revenue is mis-recorded. That's $100M in errors. We are either short-changing ourselves or our clients. This is something we need to change.
Our organisation is currently process-centric. We are restructuring to become customer-centric to better support our customers.	*The WHY is filled with buzz-word style jargon. 'Customer centric', while a great idea, is difficult to mentally visualise. What will customer-centricity mean for you and your clients?*	While we strive for great service, the reality is that our customers are often caught up in our red-tape and are stuck with a sub-par experience. From taking 5 days to respond to email and an average wait time of 60 minutes throughout our call-centres; it's clear we have much room for improvement. We can do better.

In order to comply with new legislation, we need to amend our financial reporting system.	*The WHY, while factual, is emotionally dry. While organisations can and do strive to remain law-abiding, by using some 'So-What' magic we can better call out WHY we should continue to abide by the law.*	On the 1st of July 2025 we will be liable for an estimated $1.5M p/a in penalties if we don't amend our financial reporting. This is a cost that can be easily avoided.

Notice anything about the improved WHY statements above? They are clear descriptions of the problem and/or opportunity – but they are focused on translating the why into real life. Your WHY should produce a clear visual in the reader's mind. Too many projects kick off with robotic or stale descriptions of why they exist. We shouldn't be so afraid to speak directly and with boldness.

That's how you build interest. It's how you build respect.

SO WHAT – Creating Your VQM

After we have our WHY, it's time for us to translate our WHY down our project's spine and create some important linkages. An emotional, visual WHY is great, but what does it mean for your organisation? This is the 'SO WHAT' step of our project spine, and it is answered with a Valuable Question Map (or VQM for short).

The VQM is similar to the existing industry practice of Benefits Mapping. However, there's a key difference: We eliminate the jargon, reduce the complexity and we set length limits to ensure that it's brief and to the point.

In short – we make it approachable and understandable.

Now there are a multitude of ways to do benefits mapping out there, however I've found that your traditional benefits map typically has three elements in common:

- Outputs
- Outcomes
- Benefits

Any of you who have tried to implement this type of mapping process into your organisations – you may have found that uptake was less than desired. Perhaps it even felt like a perpetual uphill battle?

While there are a number of reasons for this[20], a crucial one is the confusing use of industry jargon. Here's the test. If I gave a

---

[20] Many of which we will explore in Part 2

member of your project team(s) a piece of paper with three headings at the top of it: Outputs, Outcomes and Benefits – would they know what to write where?

My experience is that over 90% of the time they don't. This is because traditional benefits realisation management (BRM) contorts the standard meanings of these words to fit arbitrary industry rules. The words lose their self-evident nature, which is a huge issue for adoption and communication.

As a small glimpse into what I mean, let's work through a couple of these words.

Term: *Outcomes*

Dictionary Definition:

> *A result or effect of an action, situation, etc.*

How it's used in traditional benefits management:

> *An outcome is a 'loose' description of what the project is aiming to achieve. Outcomes are the positive result of change, normally affecting real world behaviour or circumstances. E.g., Improved processing capability, Higher performance system, better User Interface, etc.*

Now these definitions are somewhat close, however, outcomes in traditional BRM have a purely positive slant. So, only a minor distortion, but a distortion none the less.

But what about the term 'benefit'?

Term: *Benefit*

Dictionary Definition:

Something that is advantageous or good; an advantage.

How it's used in traditional benefits management:

The measurable improvement to the organisation as a result of achieving an outcome. It is how we know that the outcome was achieved.

And here we see one of the key challenges that traditional BRM faces. The intuitive definition of the term 'benefit' is essentially 'something good'. So, when you put this term in front of an uninitiated staff member next to the heading 'outcomes', they will get these two terms confused each and every time.

The reality is that what industry calls 'benefits' is essentially just proof. In other words, it's asking the Second Valuable Question: *"How Will We Prove It?"*.

So, in our VQM we call it that. **Proof**. Simple and without confusion. Even the explanatory text is simpler. Rather than

'The measurable improvement to the organisation as a result of achieving an outcome.'

we can use the much simpler, and jargon free:

'How do you plan to prove it?'.

And that's just one example of how the Valuable Change model creates a simpler, more useful life for you and your project staff.

So, without further ado, let's look at what makes up your VQM.

VQM Basics

First – VQM is an abbreviation. It stands for 'Valuable Question Map'.

The VQM is absolutely crucial because it's the first opportunity to answer and create connection between your project's Three Valuable Questions. It's also therefore the first opportunity to test your project's viability and logic. It's your initial sanity check. If your project doesn't make sense here, then it won't make sense moving forward. A good VQM allows you to pivot or kill off ineffective projects extremely early.

As with everything I do, the VQM is simple. So simple I can explain to you how to build one in just 2 steps.

- Step 1 – Get a piece of A4 paper or a reasonable size whiteboard.
- Step 2 – Split the paper or whiteboard into 3 columns. Label the columns as follows:
  - Column 1 – 'Why'
  - Column 2 – 'Proof'
  - Column 3 – 'What's Needed'

Congratulations you now have your blank VQM.

It should look something like this:

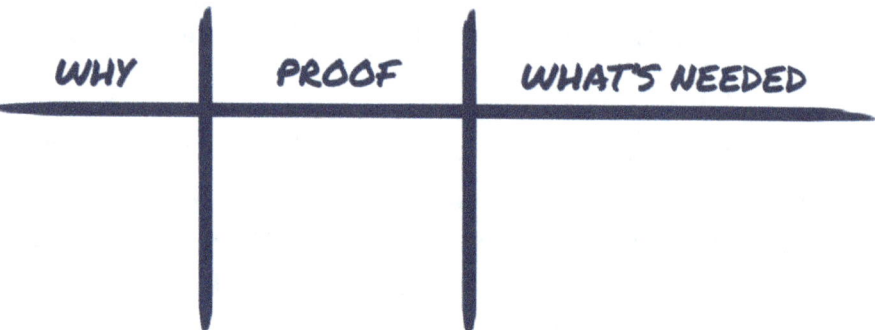

Now it's time to use it for your project. To help illustrate the process, we will work an example through the columns as we explore them.

Column 1: 'Why'

This column is where we put our answer to the first Valuable Question – *"Why Are We Doing It?"*. It draws from the core WHY (the top layer of our project spine). We represent this in summary form in this column.

So as an example, let's create a customer service transformation project. Our imaginary project has a core WHY of:

> *"While we strive for great service, the reality is that our customers are often caught up in our red-tape and are stuck with a sub-par experience.*
>
> *From taking 5 days to respond to email and an average wait time of 60 minutes throughout our call-centres; it's clear we have much room for improvement. We can do better."*

We can represent this WHY with two entries in the Core Why column, as seen in the figure below.

WHY	PROOF	WHAT'S NEEDED
REDUCED CUSTOMER RED TAPE		
IMPROVED CUSTOMER SATISFACTION		

Column 2: 'Proof'

In column 2 we answer the second Valuable Question – *"How Will We Prove It?"*. To do this we take each entry under our Core Why column and identify the key one to two ways to prove we did it. Remember the onus for proof of success sits with the project, so, this is where we specify exactly what the project is on the hook for proving.

Working through from the example above, we may end up with something like this:

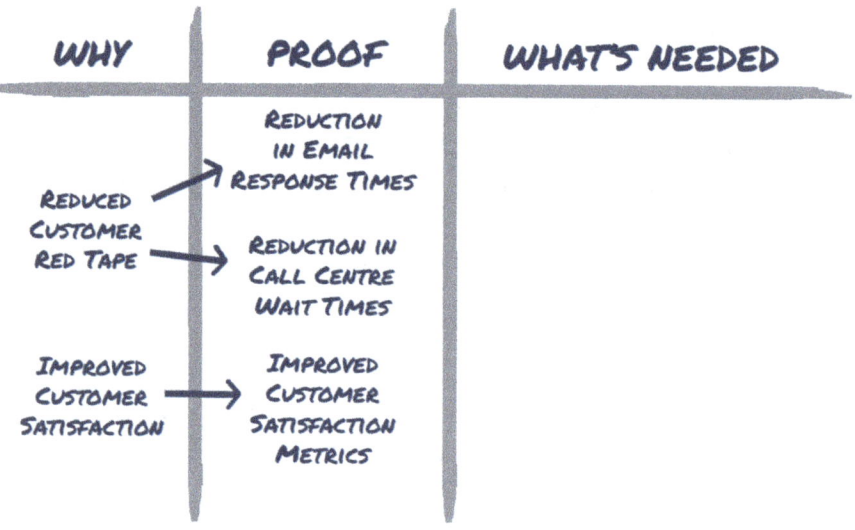

Note that we may not necessarily know what our targets for these proofs will be yet – only what we plan to demonstrate improvements in.

Column 3: 'What's Needed'

Column 3 answers our third and final Valuable Question: *"What Are We Doing?"*. We take each of those proofs and outline what needs to be done to create the desired improvements. For our worked example, this could look something like the below.

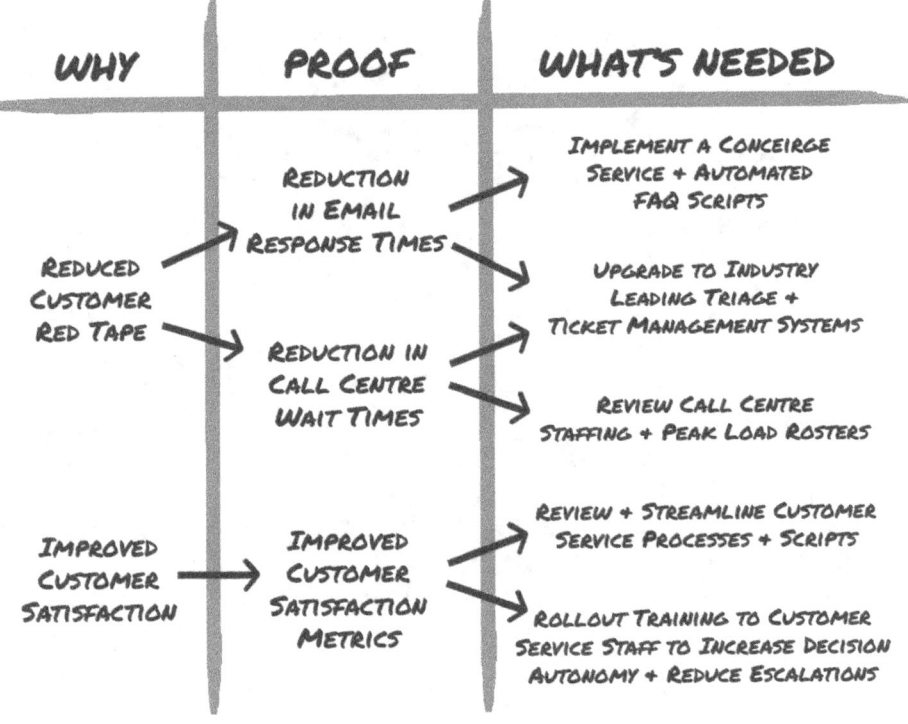

WARNING: 'ORPHAN SCOPE'

There is a huge opportunity when building your VQM to make one of the mistakes we covered last chapter. Namely Mistake 3: Answering the WHAT then Finding the WHY.

Column 3 of your VQM is the area that your staff will likely be most comfortable with. There will be a tendency to want to fill in this column first, or to just take all the current thinking on the project's scope and squish it in.

DON'T do this.

Work through each column in order. Remember that starting with WHAT you are doing, rather than the WHY is one of the fastest ways to short circuit your project's Value.

The VQM provides a sanity check on your thinking. It is how we avoid falling prey to our cognitive biases. Each connection needs to be logical, meaningful, and self-evident.

If, however, you find you have 'orphan scope', that is those things that you want to do but that don't fit in the logical flow, then I recommend two courses of action:

1. Read the section on 'The Ego Component' (Chapter 4), then
2. Re-evaluate whether you actually need to do that thing.

VQM Rules of Thumb

There are a few good practices to keep in mind when creating your VQM.

- Keep the maps as simple as possible. If it doesn't fit on one page, then you need to take it up a level.

  Note: Sometimes your change is extremely complex and expansive. If that's the case, there's nothing wrong with building an extremely high-level VQM that covers the change in its entirety, then producing a similar, more focused VQM for each of the sub-components to really track that line from WHY to WHAT.

- Proofs must be able to be measured, but you don't necessarily need to know your targets yet.

- The VQM is a 'living document', which means you should keep it up to date throughout the project. The reasons for this are simple:

    - First – it allows you to regularly revisit the logical sanity of the project.

    - Second – it allows you to easily respond to fluidity in the project executive or delivery team. A good VQM explains what your change is doing in just one page. An incredibly useful tool for anyone delivering change.

PROOF – How You Plan to Show Off

We've got our Core WHY (addressing Valuable Question 1) and, using a VQM we've outlined our answers to Valuable Questions 2 and 3. It's now time to build in some more detail, enabling us to translate our thoughts into reality. This is what we will do in PROOF (Valuable Question 2) and HOW (Valuable Question 3).

Develop a Proof Plan

Our next step towards building our project spine is to develop our Proof Plan. Once again, we aren't going to over-cook it, and we are going to avoid falling prey to industry jargon. With your Proof Plan, you will take the proofs that you identified in your VQM and add further detail, creating tangibility. Where the VQM considered the conceptual ways you plan to Prove your WHY; the Proof Plan is the data and the dates.

Here's what you need in your Proof Plan:

- The historical data for your measures,
- The future targets for your measures,
- Who is going to own and be accountable for measuring and monitoring the proofs,
- How they plan to track the proofs, and
- How you plan to respond if you start missing measurement targets.

That's it.

To give you a sense of the size of this – for a small to medium change this should only take a couple of pages to convey. Gone are the days of the 50-page benefits realisation plan.

> ## QUICK-TIP
>
> The Proof Plan contains the key things that the person(s) that fund a change should hold a change accountable to.
>
> So, make it realistic. The old adage applies. Don't oversell and underdeliver.
>
> And for those of you in charge of funding changes, note that Proof Plans only work if you keep the project accountable and ensure that the measurement goals are front of mind through the entirety of a project's life.

HOW – Answering the *'Delivery 6'*

Finally, it's time to answer Valuable Question 3: *"What are we doing?"*. This includes the WHAT and HOW of the change. In all likelihood your organisation has templates, processes, and tools for your use here. After all, most organisations are pretty good at figuring out how to deliver the WHAT. Whether this is a project plan, a project initiation document, a scoping document, or something completely different – you likely aren't starting from scratch here.

So, my advice here is simple: **Use what works**, but as always, **be wary of over-cooking.**

No matter which toolset you use to answer this question, you must ensure you are answering what I call the *'Delivery 6'*. The Delivery 6 provide key information about how you plan to go about delivering your WHY.

As this isn't a project management methodology textbook, I'll just touch on each of them briefly.

The 'Delivery 6'

1. What: "What Exactly Are We Doing?"

As we covered in Chapter 1, not enough projects have true clarity on what they are actually doing. You need to define what you plan to do, what standard it needs to achieve to be deemed 'good enough', and who is going to make that quality judgement call.

2. Approach: "How Will We Do It?"

After we define what we are doing, we then need to figure out how we will do it. With hundreds of delivery approaches prevalent across the market, you are only really limited here by the context and your imagination. The key thing to keep in mind here is that the approach needs to make sense to an outsider. If your approach makes sense, then you normally won't have much pushback on whatever you choose here.

3. Cost: "How Much Will It Cost?"

This is probably the number 1 question asked by all change executives, and for good reason. You need to know how much you expect to spend to deliver the WHAT of the Change. Estimations are never perfect so put aside money for contingencies and surprises. For most Change projects the vast majority of their spend comes from people and expertise, which leads us to the fourth question of the Delivery 6:

4. TEAM: "WHO WILL WE NEED?"

You need to have a view on who you will need to both do and administer the work. You may not necessarily have a grasp on the individuals you need, but you certainly should be able to figure out the skillsets you will require.

5. RISK: "WHAT COULD GO WRONG?"

When it comes to change projects, it can feel as if nothing ever goes to plan. While that may be an exaggeration – the successful projects are those that look ahead and ask: 'What will stop us from achieving success?'; then they plan for those events accordingly.

6. TIME: "WHEN WILL WE DO IT?"

Another favourite among organisational executives, having clarity of the when is important for both management and communication purposes. The nature of timelines differs from project to project – so the main element you need to keep in mind here is: 'What dates should my teams and stakeholders be marking on their calendars?'.

The Delivery 6 underpin your ongoing success, providing what you need to support and deliver your WHY and PROOFs.

My personal preference when it comes to answering these questions is to use a 'project one pager' that has a summary of these details all on one page. A project plan can later be developed as needed, but by producing the Delivery 6 on a one pager early on in a project's life you are able to provide much needed clarity on the WHAT. This early clarity allows a true assessment of a project's viability nice and early.

BUILDING THE CORE = A STRONG CHANGE SPINE

By now you have seen how simple and effective answering the 3 Valuable Questions can be, no matter your project. A change with a strong spine is one that is viable, logical and is well on its way to creating real value in your organisation.

Whether or not you leverage my suggested approach and toolset, the result of answering the 3 Valuable Questions by working through the Project Spine is immense.

> *BONUS FREEBIE*
> Note – as an added bonus for readers of this book, I am offering sample templates and worked examples of all of the Valuable Change Tools... for free. To claim your freebie-pack, go to *valuablechange.com/free*.

Chapter 3: Drive the Core

> *"It was like I was in a tunnel. Not only the tunnel under the hotel, but the whole circuit was a tunnel. I was just going and going, more and more and more and more. I was way over the limit but still able to find even more."*
>
> *- Ayrton Senna*

Let's take a little detour to the world of motorsport. I want to share with you what is arguably one of the greatest underdog victories of all time.

The Impossible Victory

This is the story of Tazio Nuvolari. The man who single-handedly defeated the Nazis.

I'll set the scene for you.

It's 1935.

The German Grand Prix.

The 1930s were an interesting time for grand prix racing. The cars were surprisingly powerful, running supercharged Straight-8s with over 300 brake horsepower. To give you a sense of what I'm talking about here (and for those that aren't petrol-heads) – these cars were more powerful than the 2015 editions of the top-of-the-line Volkswagen Golf or Audi S3. But unlike modern Audis or VWs, these 1935 grand prix cars were less technologically advanced than go-karts. No ABS. No traction control. No power steering. Hell, not even seatbelts.

In other words - this was driving in its rawest form.

Not only were the cars intense, but the German Grand Prix was set at the Nürburgring. For those who aren't aware of this track's fearsome reputation – the Nürburgring is still today regarded as one of the hardest tracks in the world. 174 grueling corners with over 30 metres of elevation change. Each lap is 23kms long.

In fact, in 2009, Richard Hammond of television show Top Gear fame called the Nürburgring:

> "the world's most demanding race-track."

The Nürburgring is not for the faint of heart.

Now, the Germans had set up this Grand Prix as a way to prove that they were the best in the world. The intention was for a German driver, in a German car to win the German Grand Prix. To ensure this would be the case, the Nazi party had given the two German manufacturers, Mercedes and Auto Union an extra quarter of a million Deutschmark to create bigger, more powerful engines and cutting-edge suspension systems. These cars were not only faster, but better at cornering too.

Unfortunately for Italian-bred Tazio, he wasn't in a German car. His car was a 3-year-old, technologically outdated, Alfa Romeo.

To say that the odds weren't in his favour is quite an understatement.

Race day soon arrives. The weather is miserable, and the track is damp.

The cars draw their starting positions, line up, and wait.

Bang! The race starts. The Germans all take off like lightning, leaving Tazio and his Alfa in the dust. Tazio's start is terrible, and he soon finds himself stuck in the middle of the pack.

However, he doesn't stay there for long. Unlike the other drivers, Tazio is doing something a little different. He was pioneering a new driving technique – the 4-wheel drift. Further enabled by the damp track, he was able to glide around corners that the other drivers had to wrestle through. Using the combination of this new technique and his own sheer skill, Tazio started making his way up the pack.

    5th,

    4th,

    3rd.

By Lap 6, Tazio was sitting in 2nd place. The car in front goes in for a pit stop and Tazio takes the lead!

The race continues and Tazio holds his position at the front of the pack.

It's now lap 10 and Tazio, along with the rest of the racers, is just about out of fuel. So, they all start to pit in. The Germans are in and out in under a minute. Impressively fast for 1935.

Tazio, however is not so lucky. Disaster strikes and his fuel pump breaks mid-stop! His crew scramble to find ways to get fuel into the car. Buckets, jugs and funnels fly everywhere.

Finally, the car is filled and Tazio is back on his way. The whole commotion cost him two and a half minutes – which, on a normal day would have destroyed any chance of victory in a sport that is often decided in milliseconds.

Now sitting in a futile 6th place – Tazio is enraged - so he starts to drive like a man possessed.

One by one he catches and overtakes his competitors.

His speed and approach are so intense that the other drivers are advised to *'keep clear of Tazio!'*. They fear that his pace is unsustainable, and that he is heading for disaster.

But on this day, they were wrong.

By the second to last lap, Tazio is back in 2nd place and biting at the heels of the pack leader. They enter the last lap with just 30 seconds between them.

The thing was, that gentleman in the car in front, Manfred von Brauchitsch, in his far superior Mercedes, needed tyres.

Badly...

The pressure that Tazio had kept up the entire race had meant that Manfred was pushing his own car harder than planned. This additional pressure wore out his tyres early.

But there was no time left for him to pit. With a gap of under 30 seconds (and shrinking), a pit stop would mean giving up first place. So, Manfred pushed on.

The racers fought furiously. The gap between them tightened. Tazio kept the pace high and the pressure on.

Until...

BANG!

One of the tyres on the Mercedes explodes! This gives Tazio the space he needs to take the lead.

A couple of minutes later, 300,000 German spectators look on as a lone Italian driver, in an Italian car wins the German Grand Prix. The crowd roars with the pleasure of the spectacle. The Third Reich, on the other hand, are less than impressed.

The story of Tazio's Impossible Win is a phenomenal representation of an individual's ability to truly overcome the odds.

But, there's a key problem with the picture here.

Let's take a moment to put the romanticism of the story aside. When we look at the top 10 standings from the 1935 Grand Prix, we have the following:

> 1st place – Tazio in his Alfa Romeo.
>
> 2nd place – an Auto Union car.
>
> 3rd place – a Mercedes.
>
> 4th, 5th, 6th, 7th, 8th, and 9th – all Mercedes and Auto Union.
>
> 10th place – a Maserati.

Can you see what I see?

The German manufacturers took positions 2-9. And, if it wasn't for the freak talent of Tazio, then the Germans would be holding the entirety of the top 8.

The question you need to ask yourself here is whether, in your own organisation, you would prefer to win 20% of the time based on pure organisational talent, or 80% of the time based on a superior platform. The irony here is that, even the great Tazio knew the answer to that question. He had applied to join the German Auto Union Racing Team for that 1935 season – but had been rejected.

The Power of a Better Platform

Sticking with motorsport for just a moment longer, let's ratchet forward in time to one of the most tragic and controversial seasons in the entire history of Formula One: 1994.

To combat a declining viewership and a complaint that *'technology was making the sport too predictable'*, the Fédération Internationale de l'Automobile (FIA) implemented a number of new changes for the upcoming 1994 racing season. Despite protest from the teams, the FIA instituted a ban on all electronic driver aids, such as anti-lock brakes, traction control, launch control and active suspension.

A decision that would prove to be a fatal one, with the deaths of Austrian rookie Roland Ratzenberger and three-time World Champion Ayrton Senna at the San Marino Grand Prix that year.

Amazingly, the San Marino tragedies weren't the entirety of the headlines for the season. The season was also marked with wide accusations of cheating – in particular, against the Schumacher-led Benetton team.

Cheating allegations begun at the very first race of the 1994 season, the Brazilian Grand Prix. The Benetton pit crew had made a pit-stop that was just a little 'too quick' – giving Schumacher the lead. Speculation soon arose that Benetton was using a system to make quicker pit stops than their rivals.

From that point, cheating allegations arose regularly throughout the season, from illegal use of traction control, to hidden launch software triggers, automated gearboxes and fuel system tampering which ultimately resulted in a large fire mid-race.

But here's the bottom line. Despite these allegations, and several race bans, the Schumacher-led Benetton still won the championship.

If nothing else, 1994 shows us the opposite side of that 1935 race. What happens when operating at breakneck speeds relying solely on personal performance? Tragedy.

The team that stood victorious was the one that, (allegedly) continued to tip the scale in their favour with the use of driver's aids. They didn't rely solely on their driver's personal talent[21].

Thankfully in our organisations we aren't plagued with declining *'change viewership'*, nor are we incentivised to make things *'more exciting'*. Our goals are closer to the Benetton team's ones: **'Consistent Success'.**

So, what does that mean for our change initiatives?

We must create an organisational platform that best positions our teams to deliver truly Valuable Change consistently. This means installing as many driver's aids[22] as we possibly can.

---

[21] Of which Michael Schumacher has plenty.
[22] I use the terms driver's aids and driver's assists interchangeably throughout the rest of this book.

And, while we don't have traction control or fuel filters to contend with – our variables are still equally important for ensuring maximum speed on our way to consistent success.

Our variables are our:

- Decisions,
- Habits, and
- Documentation.

Oh, and a quick side note. Some of my early reviewers thought I may have been recommending cheating here.

I'm not.

Almost every one of the driver's aids that Schumacher may or may not have used is installed in all modern cars. We aren't cheating when we drive down the road to go pick up a carton of milk. We are, however, able to drive faster with confidence because of them.

The point here is not one of 'cheating to win', but rather one of building a better change platform by installing more effective driver's aids.

DRIVER AID 1: VALUABLE DECISIONS

"Whenever you see a successful business, someone once made a courageous decision"

- Peter F. Drucker

It's time to talk about the most important element of your Valuable Change Platform: Valuable Decision Making.

Courage (or cowardice) when making decisions will make or break your change success.

Let's do a little mental exercise. Bring into your mind a project or program that you may have worked on, led, or merely spectated that meets one or more of the following criteria:

- It never ended,
- It caused more pain than gain,
- It didn't solve the original problem or meet the original need,
- It regularly surprised its stakeholders,
- It was filled with 'last minute scrambles', or
- It had no way of proving success (although it may well have claimed it was 'successful').

Got a project in mind? Great.

Now reflect on the way decisions were made in that project. Would you say that the decisions were cowardly or courageous? Here's a few hints.

Were decisions deferred until the last minute?

Were decisions made as knee-jerk reactions?

Were decision makers sufficiently across the issues, or was it closer to shooting in the dark[23]?

So, what makes a decision courageous?

As always with me, it's simple:

> *A courageous decision is one that chooses the harder right over the easier (or even harder) wrong.'*

Unfortunately, we aren't operating in a comic book universe. Saying 'choose the right' would be foolishly naïve. Reality, especially when changing organisations, is filled with shades of grey. These shades of grey often leave us in difficult spots – which logically brings us to the real question here:

> *'How do we ensure we make the best decision?'*

Now, there are millions of books about decision making. Each with its own 'decision process', with variations from 3 to 10 steps. Thankfully, this isn't one of those books. I prefer a different, simpler approach: **Make it as easy as possible**. To do this, we must first consider what makes a decision hard to make? There are two key elements at play here:

Data and Emotion.

When we plot those out, we get the Decision Difficulty Quadrant (shown below). Any decision where we have low data and low

---

[23] Something I have personally done while doing my firearms safety course. I can assure you, shooting a .22 down a pitch-black gun range is completely ineffective.

emotion will be no better than gauging the weather by putting our finger in the air or throwing a dart with a blindfold on.

Any decision with high emotion and low data is probably wrong.

Any decision with low emotion and high data is as simple as connecting the dots or just doing what the data tells you to do.

And, finally, any decision made with high data and high emotion is likely one that will be tough, but necessary.

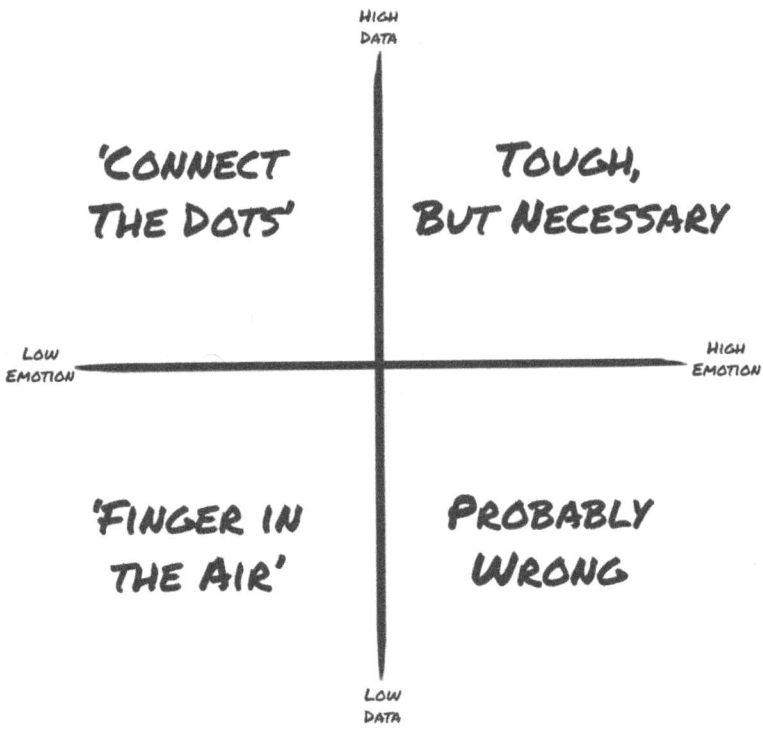

In other words, the easiest decisions we can make are the 'connect the dot' style decisions: lots of clear, useful data and low levels of emotion attached.

The hardest are those that are the opposite – unclear data and lots of emotion. We don't often get those ones right.

So, how do we make our decisions easier?

Like the formula one drivers at the start of this chapter – we install drivers' aids.

I'm going to assume that we are all relatively emotionally stable, and that we are neither automatons nor sociopaths. This means that the quickest way to improve our decisions is to increase our data.

But here's the thing - it's not just any data.

Truly Valuable Change requires setting up the mechanisms to continuously inform and predict the answers to the mid-flight variations of our 3 Valuable Questions[24]:

1. Does it still make sense?
2. What do our early indicators say?
3. Are we progressing as expected?

---

[24] As discussed in Chapter 1.

DOES THE CHANGE STILL MAKE SENSE?

In Chapter 1 we talked about the one-two punch of the first Valuable Question, that is, Why Are We Doing It?

Well, it's time for that second punch – *Does This Still Make Sense?*

Or, to put it another way, is the project WHY still valid?

The art is in the ongoing validation of the WHY. A great way to think about this is in terms of *'proof of the problem'*. To leverage a previous example, that could look something like the below:

PROJECT WHY	PROOF OF THE PROBLEM	Y/N
THE CURRENT SYSTEM IS CLUNKY + SLOW	– IS THE SYSTEM STILL IN USE?	Y/N
	– DOES THE SYSTEM STILL TAKE >5 SECONDS TO LOAD SIMPLE TRANSACTIONS?	Y/N
	– ARE USER MISTAKES STILL HIGHER THAN 12%?	Y/N

This is a prime example of where the right data makes the decision easier. The decision shifts from a wish-wash of general feeling into one of three options:

a) The WHY is still valid,
b) The WHY landscape is changing and needs exploration and monitoring, or
c) The WHY is no longer valid.

This gives decision makers for Valuable Change programs a streamlined and simple decision tree:

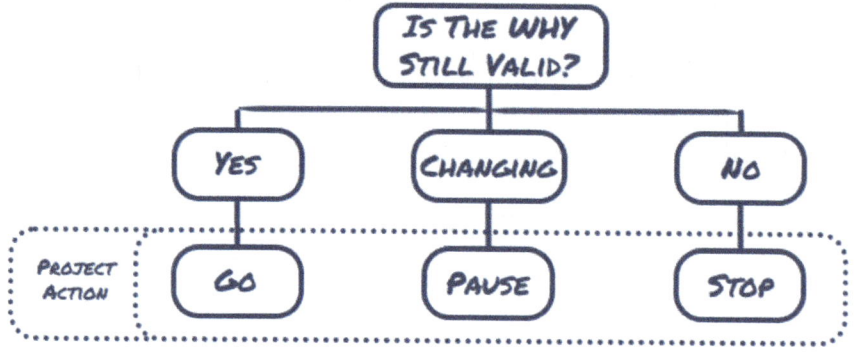

WHAT DO OUR EARLY INDICATORS SAY?

The 'in-flight' extension of our second Valuable Question (How Will We Prove It?) is '*What Do Our Early Indicators Say?*'

There is a common objection to the idea of looking at proof data throughout a project. It's that:

> 'the benefits will all be realised at the end'.

But this objection falls over when you apply some logical creativity[25]. For the vast majority of your planned proof metrics, you can either get direct data mid-project or, as a minimum put something in place to provide early indication of what the eventual proofs may be.

---

[25] A beautiful oxymoron.

Here's a few examples, but this, in no way, forms an exhaustive list as each change is different.

Proof	Potential Early Indicator
Better Customer Experience	→ Initial Focus Group Results
System Outage Reduction	→ Performance Testing Results
Cost Savings	→ Current / Projected Reductions
Increased Revenue	→ Market Testing Results

Once you have early indicators in place, then the decision flow is nice and simple.

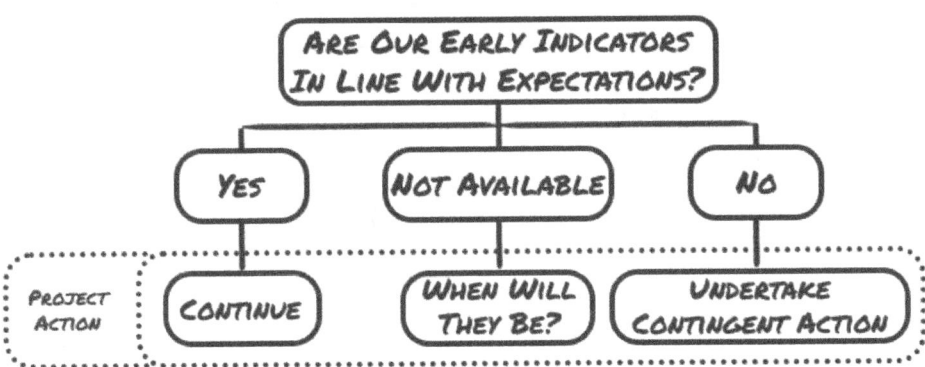

ARE WE PROGRESSING AS EXPECTED?

Finally, we have '*Are We Progressing as Expected*'?

Across the vast majority of projects this is the only question of the 3 that is actually answered. (Mirroring the same heavy delivery-focus we discussed in Chapter 2). This question is often termed 'project status' and is normally represented using what I call '*project status soup*' - a mix of Red, Amber, Green indicators for a mix of variables spanning Time, Cost, Risk, Issues, Quality, Resources, Dependencies, Scope, Governance and many more.

At the risk of sounding blasphemous here, but in a revelation that is probably no surprise to anyone – the industry is again over complicating it.

In essence this question has 2 key parts[26]:

a) Are we progressing as expected?
   Y/N
b) Do we expect to continue to progress as expected?
   Y/N

Again, the right data is your friend here. Pick the metrics that are most important for your change, those which a failure to hit would invalidate the viability of solving the project's WHY. Then monitor them.

---

[26] There you go, I just simplified your project reports to just 2 binary indicators, and probably a dot point comment field. You can thank me later.

Cost and Time are the most common-sense selections here. There is no need to track 11 different variations of what are essentially just potential or current threats.

Like the other questions we have discussed, the decision flow is simple.

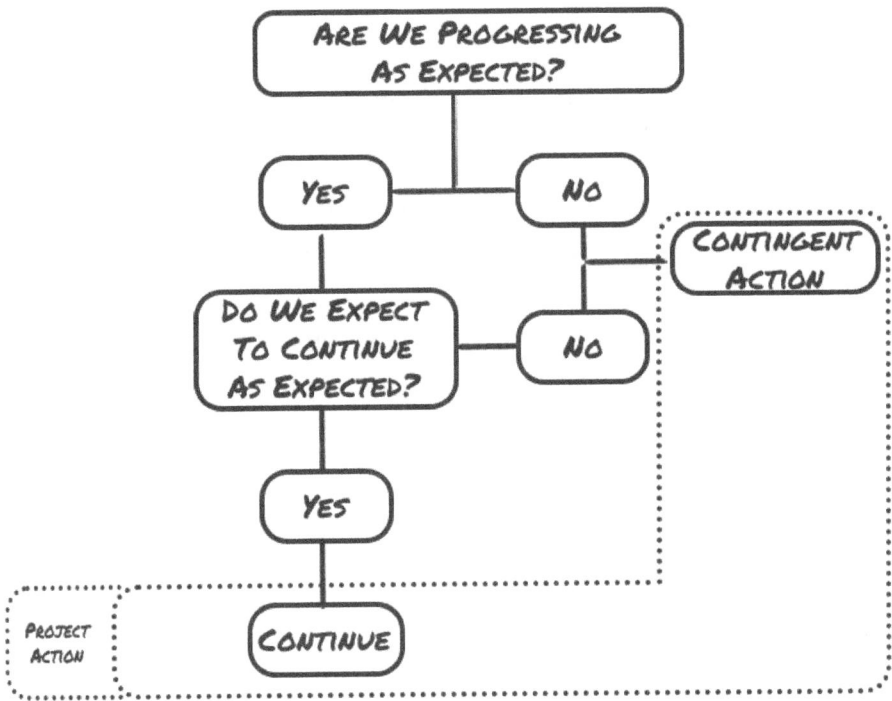

THE ROLE OF VALUABLE DECISIONS

Valuable Decision making provides a crucial driver's aid for your Valuable Change Platform. Put simply, it helps ensure ongoing alignment.

- Alignment with your organisation's need,
- Alignment with what the data is telling you, and
- Alignment with what is next needed to achieve the core change WHY.

A Valuable Change is continuously aware of its environment, it's trajectory and its progress. The easiest way to achieve this is to install this information as ongoing data-driven 'driver aids' to make decision making as close to a 'follow the dots' experience for you and other decision makers as possible.

Driver Aid 2: The Learning Habit

"Quality is not an act, it is a habit."

- Aristotle

By now we all know the power of habit. There's even a New York Times bestseller with that exact title. So, let's talk about the three key habits that your organisation must be able to do well to ensure ongoing improvement:

1) It must be able to fail, and learn,
2) It must be able to succeed, and learn, and
3) It must be able to share and make forecasts using those learnings.

So really, those 3 habits are just one.

A habit of learning.

Yes, that old nutshell – Learning.

We usually love to do it.

But... we usually don't love the work involved to get it.

The key question here is how do we embed learning into our teams, and then, maximise the payoff of doing so?

Now, if you have been around projects for a while then you will likely be well versed in the idea of a 'lesson learned'. For those of you that haven't been in projects for a while, here's a quick summary: When projects get to a key closure point (whether that be the end of an iteration, a stage or the entire project), the project team will sit back and reflect on what went well, and what didn't. The idea is that these reflections and learnings can then be passed forward to future projects to improve their chances of success.

The issue is – people aren't doing it.

3 Levels of Learning

To help you visualise and self-assess how well your organisation, team or project is learning, you should evaluate yourself against 3 levels:

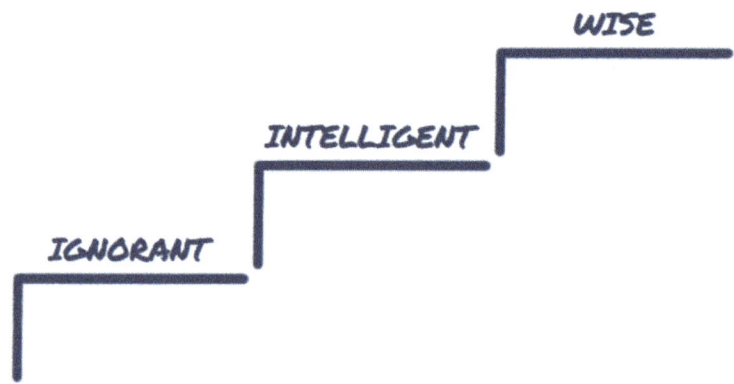

Level 1: Ignorant

The first level, and unfortunately the one that is most common, is one of Ignorance. This is one time that ignorance isn't bliss... An organisation that is Ignorant keeps making the same mistakes over and over and over again. The problem is, it may not know it's doing so. There is no conscious effort, time or money dedicated to reviewing, reflecting or learning from the past. Any learnings that are integrated are stored in your long-term employees' heads - and leaves when they do.

This is a major problem facing most organisations deploying a modern, fluid workforce. But it is orders of magnitude worse for our change initiatives because by nature there is almost always a temporary staff arrangement. From external contractors, fly-in consultants, or internal secondments; there's often a LOT of learning that walks out the door during and after a change.

Level 2: Intelligent

Or maybe your organisation isn't ignorant. Maybe it does see the value in capturing learnings at the end of key projects or during periodic reviews.

And maybe your organisation is sitting on a veritable goldmine of knowledge. Spread throughout your digital filing system there may well be minutes of lessons workshops, notes from retrospectives, project status and closure reports, risk & issue reviews, and more.

Or maybe your organisation even goes so far as to consolidate these into a list... somewhere... that if you ran a document search for... you *might* be able to find.

If any of the above sounds familiar, then your organisation, team or change initiative is Intelligent. By this I mean you have lots of knowledge at your fingertips, but you aren't translating that into real action and growth.

Level 3: Wise

Now, for a slim number of you, you may have read the descriptions of the previous two levels and thought to yourself:

"No, we're doing better than that".

And if you did, then I truly commend you. You could be operating at the top level: Wise.

Organisations, teams and projects that are Wise are able to connect the dots. By this I mean that they have created a clear path from reflection -> lesson capture -> lesson implementation. Whether outwardly or subtly, organisations that are wise have embedded the difference between a *'lesson logged'* and a *'lesson learned'*. Further these organisations have embedded learning into their regular processes, and it's become *just part of what they do'*. And these processes don't just include reflection, but also sharing and prediction. The net result of which is a genuine improvement at their next attempt at whatever it is they are attempting. So, let's spend a little time exploring the 2 key elements that need to be in place to take any organisation from Ignorant to Wise.

The First Wise Element: Normalise Failure, Success and Reflection

The first element that must be in place for our new learning habit is a culture of openness.

...I know.

Easier said than done, right?

I'm guessing you've heard the age-old question – what came first, the chicken or the egg[27]? Well, there's another version that's perhaps even trickier:

> 'What came first, the culture or the ritual?'

Whichever side of the fence you're on though, the answer really doesn't matter because despite claims to the contrary, you can't implement a new culture. What you can do, however, is implement new organisational rituals. So, that's where we are going to focus our attention.

There are three key areas we need to target to create a culture of openness. All three are centred on normalising what are typically difficult things. They are: Failure, Success, and Reflection.

---

[27] In case you were wondering, it was the egg. Eggs were used by various life forms millions of years before the chicken (as we know it) existed.

NORMALISING FAILURE

First, reader, I have a question for you. When was the last time you truly failed? By this I mean gut wrenching, plate smashing, sleep destroying failure.

Has it been a while? Or perhaps it's fresh and you are still sore from it? Either way, I bet you learned something valuable that you now share with others.

This is acute failure.

Acute failure is useful. We tend to create real behavioural shifts from it because we are often forced to. Acute failure is effective – but acute failure is expensive.

Interestingly, acute failure is what we often think about when we think of failure. So, when someone says to you that you should *'embrace failure',* most of the time people tend to think of recovering better from acute failure.

But, what about the other type of failure? The subtle, everyday stuff. The comment that went over wrong at the meeting yesterday. The workshop that went 30 minutes overtime. The decision to buy fast food instead of bringing something pre-prepared from home.

Subtle failure is insidious, it adds up, but it doesn't cause notable behavioral change. It lingers. Subtle failures hardly ever see the light of day. No reflection, no storytelling, no growth.

This is the stuff that often slowly undermines your teams. And it is both the acute and the subtle failure that we need to try to normalise.

The great news is that it's relatively easy to do.

Create a *failure session* at the end of a day or week to provide the space and opportunity for your team(s) to expose their failures. The agenda of a failure session typically looks something like this:

1) Tell us all a story of something that went terribly wrong today/this week, and some quick advice for your teammates from that experience. (30-45 seconds max per person).
2) Repeat for the next person.

The agenda isn't groundbreaking, however it's the follow-up activity that's really powerful here. After the reflection point, write everyone's failure and advice on a white board (or similar) that is visible to all for the following day/week.[28]

Ensure the session is lighthearted, and that everyone gets a chance to share. However, a quick word of warning here. Do NOT ever let this session become a confirmation of failures or an opportunity to condescend and criticise. The space must be safe and fun.

---

[28] If any of the failures/advice are directly project or work related, you may want to get them noted into a form that is later searchable.

Through the simple act of exposure, lighthearted storytelling and a little public accountability, failure becomes normal. When failure is normal, openness increases.

Normalising Success

Interestingly, the polar opposite of failure also needs normalisation. This is primarily due to the too-common fear of being cut down – often called Tall Poppy Syndrome[29]. The result of a team or individual suffering from Tall Poppy Syndrome is an aversion to risk, not because they are afraid of the risk going wrong – but rather they are afraid of the risk going right!

The problem here is that anyone implementing change is in an inherently risky position. When you are rowing upstream, your team(s) need to have the open and ongoing support of their colleagues.

So, to normalise success, we can again use a simple team gathering.

This time, it's a celebration of sorts – I call these *'Blow Your Own Horn'* sessions. After all, as Alan Weiss says,

> *"If you don't blow your own horn, there is no music."*

A Blow Your Own Horn (BYOH) session is a regular opportunity for your team(s) to meet and safely discuss the achievements they are most proud of that week.

The rules for a BYOH session are simple:

---

[29] We cover Tall Poppy Syndrome in more detail in Chapter 5.

- Only one person speaks at a time.
- Everyone must share at least one thing they are proud of that week.
- They should speak boldly and be free to boast. Storytelling and hyperbole are acceptable.
- These are not feedback sessions, successes are celebrated, never refuted.

As you roll these out, there will be an initial awkwardness over the first few meetings as people adjust to the new self-promotional norm. This is where you, as a Valuable Change leader, must lead by example. Be candid and bold with what you share. BYOH sessions attack the fears within your teams by providing each of them social permission to grow.

A QUICK NOTE ON SOCIAL PERMISSION

A situation I see far too often is energised individuals (especially those new to a team or project) with great ideas, shrinking into a general monotony in just a few weeks. Their creative light diminished. Instead of being harnessed and embraced – new energy is squandered and suppressed. The underlying cause of this is a lack of Social Permission. Individuals are not given explicit permission to grow, and so they wilt. It's our job as a leader to empower and enable boldness.

Normalising Reflection – Learning Journeys

The final uncomfortable thing we need to normalise is reflection – in particular, group reflection.

Hands up if you've ever sat in one of those awkward lesson review sessions at the end of change initiative, bored out of your mind, being asked the same old questions:

- What went well?
- What could we have done better?

Typically, these are framed against a series of categories. Time, Cost, Quality, Governance, and the like.

What's worse, is that unless it's a particularly dynamic team, everyone in attendance is usually super quiet, bar a couple of loudmouths who are either a) all too happy to rip the project to shreds, or b) paint an uncomfortably pretty picture of reality.

There are two issues at play here:

1) Most people aren't comfortable sharing their reflections in one arbitrary session at the end of a project when most of the time nothing they say is going to make a difference, and
2) There's normally an overwhelmingly one-sided perception of a project's success, whether that be positive or negative.

Here's how to have a different conversation.

Tell a group story. A Learning Journey.

Now, I'm not going to claim credit for this idea, but unfortunately, I can't recall where I came across it. However, I would be remiss if I didn't share it with you as it's a technique that I've well and truly adopted into my own toolbox. The theory here is simple. We humans have communicated through story for as long as we have been human. Tap into this tradition by collaboratively telling the story of your change effort over the last week, month or quarter. Rather than trying to remember what went well - create an interactive, evolving plotline. To do so, create a shared space for your team with a simple straight line.

Something like the below.

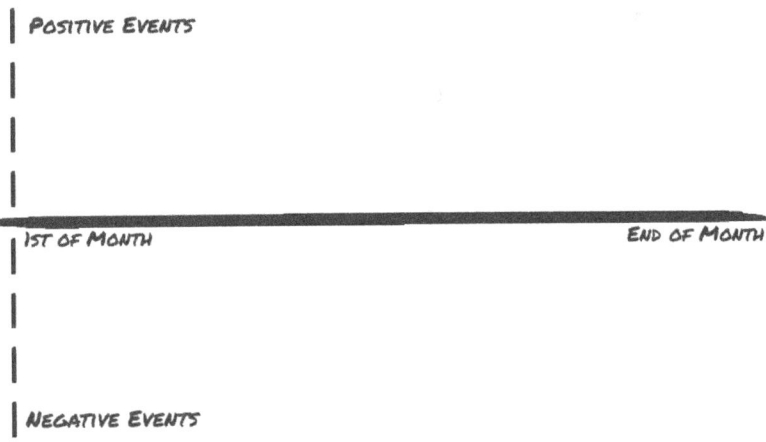

Then as the month[30] progresses, encourage your team to tell the story of your project on your interactive plotline. As an example, maybe you are 10 days into the month and your plotline is shaping up like the following.

---

[30] Or whatever time period makes sense for your initiative.

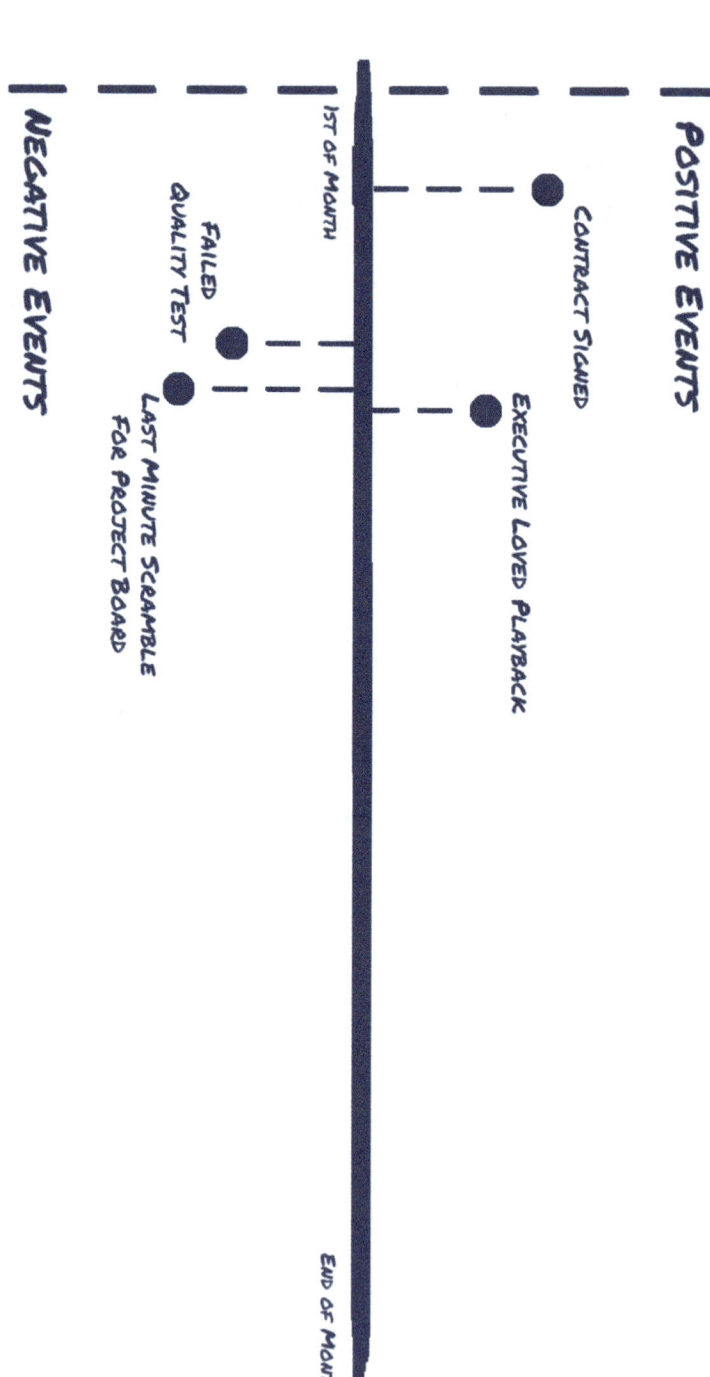

I'm sure you can see the power of this. No more pulling lessons from people like you would pull teeth. This plotline tells the story of your change initiative. Its highs, its lows. Ultimately, as you progress you will be identifying lessons as you are experiencing them.

Here's a few tips on Learning Journeys:

- When first introducing this practice, there is value in prompting and eliciting plot points in your daily standups or similar regular team meetings.
- Toward the end of the story period, you can hold a session to translate the plot into potential learnings.

The Second Wise Element: Proof, Sharing and Prediction

The second element we must have in place to become a Wise organisation is a focus on proof, sharing and prediction.

Proof

If you're this far into the book, then you likely already understand the importance of proof. A proof's importance doesn't suddenly stop when we talk about our organisation's learning. The crucial idea here is:

Writing a lesson down doesn't mean that we've learnt it.

What I'm saying here is that Identification ≠ Proof.[31]

Just because we sat back and said:

> *"We could have done XYZ, which would have created a better result."*

is no guarantee that you or your successors won't repeat the same mistake in the future. A better frame for our Learning effort is one that creates a separation between identification and learning. I often term these a Lesson Logged vs a Lesson Learned. But feel free to adjust the language as you see fit. What is important here is the frame.

Learning requires action, and ultimately, learning requires proof.

---

[31] That is, Identification doesn't equal proof.

And how do we get proof?

We help others avoid our mistakes by sharing our lessons.

SHARING

OK, let's talk a little about sharing.

Yes, that thing your parents (probably) drilled into you when you were a child, especially if you had siblings. But there's a key difference between sharing learnings and sharing a toy. Sharing a lesson doesn't mean you don't get to play with it too - it just multiplies the knowledge.

This is a vastly overlooked point in almost every organisation.

Sharing multiplies knowledge!

Your people are limited. You share a resource; you lose that capacity for as long as they are shared. It's a net neutral position for the organisation.

They gain 1, you lose 1.

Similarly, your capital is limited. You share your change funds; you no longer have use of those funds for your own change initiative. Again, a net neutral position.

They gain $100k, you lose $100k.

Yet when you share your knowledge, your learnings, you don't lose anything. It's a net positive position for the organisation.

They gain knowledge yet you lose nothing.

This is why sharing our learnings is so important. There are a number of ways to do this, and your organisation will have its own preference. I've seen all sorts of things work here. From internal Wikis, closed Facebook pages, SharePoint lists, intranet knowledge hubs, lunch and learns, and concierge 'lesson search' Project Office services – it all works.

The method isn't as important as the actual act of sharing. Just remember that it's not sharing if no one knows it's available.

PREDICTION

Prediction is the final stage for any organisation focused on learning. It's the culmination of every element we've already discussed. Prediction is what happens when an organisation combines forward planning with knowledge of the past to create better change. Like lesson sharing, prediction takes many forms, but can be used within both new and in-place change initiatives.

The two most common approaches are:

1) Creating 'typical project' profiles along with the common roadblocks and opportunities that project can expect to face, and
2) Monitoring staff estimation ability, comparing initial estimates to actual results – reviewing the lessons learned in the process to further refine that skill.

CREATING EXPONENTIAL LEARNING

Have you ever heard the phrase:

'This will multiply your results ten-fold'?

Well, here's a little secret. True organisational learning leaves ten-fold in the dust.

Due to the net-positive effect of knowledge sharing we explored a few pages ago, **embedding the Learning Habit into our change efforts puts into place exponential levels of improvement**. It can be as effective as a multi-level-marketing scheme, but notably less dubious.

When an organisation is open to success and failure, tells stories, shares learnings, improves predictions, and focuses on proof… well, let's just say creating Valuable Change is that much easier.

In other words - Learning is a phenomenal driver's aid when you're in the driver's seat.

Driver Aid 3: Simplest Practical Artefacts (SPAs)

The final driver aid we will discuss here are *SPAs: Simplest Practical Artefacts*.

The theory behind these is dead simple:

Ensure every artefact (every document, form, checklist, or 'thing by any other name') meets 3 key checks:

- It has a clear purpose.
- It covers what it must to meet the purpose.
- It covers no more than it must to meet that purpose.

Those 3 simple rules eliminate most of the duplication and overwhelm that our change initiatives face when it comes to documentation and process. In the next chapter we will explore the Value Equation, the key takeaway of which is that we must look for ways to maximise reward and minimise pain. This pain minimisation is especially important when it comes to documentation. Too often I see change frameworks that ask the same questions over and over in different but similar forms. In fact, there's a quick hint here – if there is any content that your project managers are copying and pasting between documents, then you aren't using simplest practical artefacts.

TECHNIQUES TO ACHIEVING SIMPLEST PRACTICAL

Getting to 'Simplest Practical' is an ongoing effort but can be greatly helped by a series of techniques. These are:

- Connect Question to Purpose,
- Think Modular,
- Ask - Is This Even Necessary,
- Cost Visualisation, and a
- Bonus Technique: Mystery Shopping

Let's touch on each one individually.

CONNECT QUESTION TO PURPOSE

Now, if you're one to pick up on patterns, then you might have noticed a common theme throughout this book.

That is, I have a particular liking for questions.

More specifically – asking the right ones.

And here lies the first step to creating the Simplest Practical Artefacts: It's the questions that you are asking.

...And there are plenty of questions to ask!

When we are kicking off a new change initiative, we want to be asking our 3 Valuable Questions:

1) Why are we doing it?
2) How will we know we are successful? (And how will we prove it?)
3) What are we doing?

Then of course number 3 breaks into our Delivery 6:

    a. What exactly are we doing?

    b. How will we do it?

    c. How much will it cost?

    d. Who will we need?

    e. What could go wrong?

    f. When will we do it?

Once we are mid-change our questions adapt, and we are now focused on:

1) Does this still make sense, and is the WHY still valid?
2) What do the early indicators say?
3) Are we progressing as expected?
4) Do we expect to continue to progress as expected?
5) What are we learning?

Then finally our questions adapt again once our change has been operationalised.

1) Were we successful?

2) What does our proof say?

3) What now needs to be done?

Now, of course this list of questions isn't exhaustive. There will be many more questions to be answered that depend entirely on the type of change and your context.

The art in getting to Simplest Practical is in ensuring that you don't ask the same question several times.

You want to create this:

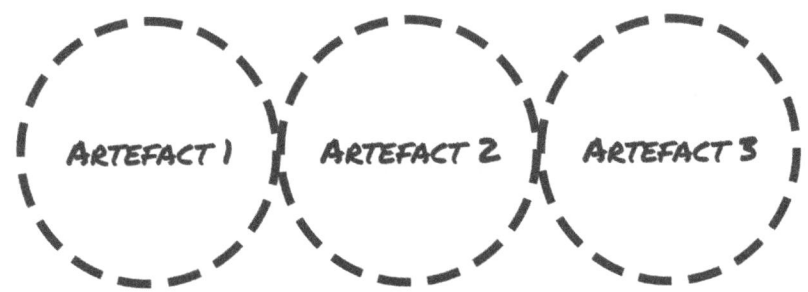

Not this:

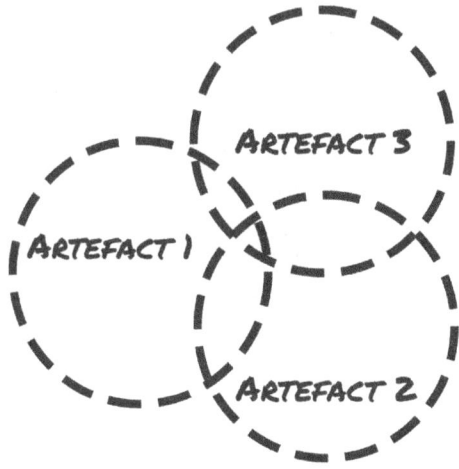

The surest and simplest way to achieve that is to directly link your artefact's purpose with the question it's answering.

THINK MODULAR

The fact is that 6 x 1-page documents are shorter and more flexible than one 30 page one. This is the power of modular thinking.

No more *'single document to rule them all',* rather, you're better off having clear and direct answers to key change questions. This saves both the writer and the reader time, and comes with the added bonus of making the communication clearer.

ASK - IS THIS EVEN NECESSARY?

To create Simplest Practical Artefacts you must ask a key question (Yes, I know... I did tell you I liked questions).

You must ask: *'Is This Even Necessary'?*

It seems almost silly on first blush. After all, why in the world would you have artefacts that you don't need?

But for anyone reading this book that's been around change for a little while, you're probably nodding your head here. Across my client engagements, by asking this simple question we always find an artefact or three that are just plain unnecessary.

So, we kill them[32] off.

You should too.

COST PERSPECTIVE

The final technique is one of cost-perspective. That is, does the effort and cost to the organisation of preparing this artefact make sense and feel reasonable?

Here's a very real example of this at play.

If I gave you an additional $560,000 a year, what would you do with it?

...Probably not this.

---

[32] The artefacts I mean. Thankfully, I haven't been asked to work as a hitman by any client yet.

A portfolio manager was producing an organisation-wide project summary report on a quarterly basis. Unfortunately for this manager, the report was often bumped off her Executives' busy agenda. It was a tick and flick activity for the Executives who each viewed the report as low value, low pain.

What wasn't seen by these Executives was the pain in getting to that point. When you tallied the 40+ project managers' time and the multiple quality assurance steps this client's team undertook on the report – the organisation was wearing in excess of $140,000 each quarter to produce this routinely ignored report[33].

It was also a dreaded activity for all involved and distracted focus away from the delivery of the already in-flight projects.

Comically, this manager was considering doubling down on the pain and producing the report monthly!

Simplest Practical Artefacts are cost-proportional to their purpose. A simple trick here is the addition of an 'estimated cost to produce/complete' metric to your artefacts. On face value, it can be hard to see the time, effort and therefore the cost of a document or similar. By exposing this information, you will be placing the Return on Investment of the artefact under scrutiny. This is a GOOD thing.

---

[33] Among other strategies, placing a 'cost to produce' metric on the report notably reduced the executive bump rate.

> ### *SIMPLEST PRACTICAL MEETINGS*
>
> Everything we have just discussed for Simplest Practical Artefacts can and should also be applied to your meetings. Meetings are a bugbear for many organisations, and don't need to be.
>
> And if you haven't yet explored the use of a 'live meeting cost calculator', then I would encourage you to. Watching the dollars tick by is a great way to shorten your meetings and keep people on point.

BONUS TECHNIQUE: MYSTERY SHOPPING

OK, so let's say you have a nice clear purpose for each artefact – which is linked to a clear question. You have also identified a couple of artefacts that just weren't needed.

Now what?

Well, here's a little bonus technique for you.

Artefact & Process Mystery Shopping.

Have you ever wondered how Bunnings Warehouse, the largest and most prevalent home improvement retailer in Australia, continues to grow and improve its customer service over the years?

In truth the answer is multi-faceted, but continuous improvement driven by mystery shopping is a large part of it. Bunnings Warehouse are obsessed with a customer's experience, and accordingly pay meticulous attention to it.

Now, if you have ever worked in or around retail, then you are probably comfortable with the idea of a Mystery Shop. For those of you that haven't here's a quick summary: Retail managers are often concerned about the quality of their store's customer service, so they hire externals to come and shop at their store. These externals then evaluate each key step of their shopping experience.

> Were they greeted by an assistant as they entered the store?
>
> Were they provided useful advice?
>
> Was checkout particularly difficult?

The mystery shoppers never reveal themselves to staff, and the staff aren't usually even told that mystery shoppers are coming.[34] The evaluations are then considered, and key pain points identified and remedied.

So, how does this help a Valuable Change practitioner?

If you haven't already guessed, I'm suggesting a little ninja work here. Mystery Shop your own documents and processes. Enlist

---

[34] Although, some particularly sneaky managers may let slip that 'mystery shoppers are coming over the next month' to put their staff on edge and up their job performance over that period.

staff outside your control to test out and evaluate your processes & artefacts, and along the way have them evaluate how they are feeling about it.

...I know, it may sound a little esoteric here, but stay with me.

In the next chapter we will talk about Reward vs Pain. Your mystery shopper's feelings provide you early indication of the type of pain your processes are causing. If your mystery shopper starts to feel frustration, anger or even exhaustion -> then your artefacts and processes likely have duplication or unnecessary requirements. An iteration or three of this mystery shopping and you will be operating with slim, simple, and practical artefacts.

> ## A SAD TRUTH
>
> Here's a sad truth. Most people that read the above section about Mystery Shoppers will think *"Wow, that's pretty cool. It's a shame it just wouldn't work for my artefacts and processes."* And so, it just stays a cool idea. Nothing more.
>
> Ultimately, it's the bold that will inherit the true success that Valuable Change can bring. So next time you find yourself thinking "That won't work for me" I challenge you – think instead: **"How can I have that work for me?"**

The Truth About Driver's Aids

The truth about driver's aids is that there are multitudes you could choose from. In this chapter I've provided three that are so simple you could implement them tomorrow, and of course I encourage you to do so. But ultimately the message of this chapter is a simple one.

Build a better platform. Ensuring you embed the core of your change into it.

Don't just rely on your star performers, the 'Tazio Nuvolari's' of your organisation. Find ways to give all your drivers unfair advantages. Bigger engines. Better suspension. Slicker tyres. Faster fuel pumps.

Make driving fast easier for them.

Then let them drive you to victory.

PART TWO: YOUR PEOPLE

Chapter 4: Stack The Value Equation

"There is a thin line that separates laughter and pain, comedy and tragedy, humor and hurt."

- Erma Bombeck

Why We Do Things (Or Don't)

(Anecdotally), 95% of change initiatives require someone, somewhere to do something new or different.

Sometimes this someone does do the new thing.

And sometimes they don't.

The reasons given for this vary. Trust me, I've heard them all. There was a lack of executive support. It was a bad user experience. Teams were engaged too late. We were too busy.

No matter the reason given, there's really only one true answer that consistently explains why someone didn't do something.

There just wasn't enough value.

So, what differentiates a change that sticks and one that doesn't?

The Value Equation.

The Value Equation underpins your change success. It applies no matter the type of change you are looking to drive.

New process? Tick.

New system? Tick.

New behaviours? Tick.

New location? Tick.

New culture? Tick.

It applies no matter the change, because it's the reason why people do things (and why they don't).

Thankfully, the Value Equation is simple. It only has 3 parts:

1) The reward you receive for doing something.
2) The pain you must endure to get the reward.
3) The net result of the reward minus the pain, ultimately determining your decision to pursue the reward, or not.

You can think of it as an equation like this:

REWARD − PAIN = DECISION

Or you can think of it as two columns, a little like the classic 'pros vs cons' decision-making approach.

Now on first glance the Value Equation seems self-evident[35], but there's some interesting science behind it.

---

[35] I warned you of the self-evident nature of the book all the way back in my author's intro.

The Interesting Science Behind It

Over the last half century behavioural studies of those suffering chronic pain have found that we humans will actively avoid any activity that we fear will result in a painful experience.

No surprises there.

However, in 2012 a group of behavioural scientists at Ghent University in Belgium felt that the current pain-avoidance thinking was too narrow. They hypothesised that the findings to date on pain-avoidance were sorely[36] one sided; and that the decision to avoid or persist with a painful activity is likely affected by the level of motivational conflict at the point of decision. In short - **we only avoid pain if we don't have a good reason to endure it.**

So, they put together an experiment[37], and like all good experiments, it included zapping people. After gaining approval from the Ghent University's ethical committee – they were good to go.

56 undergraduate students volunteered to participate in the experiment and were split into two groups.

The first group of poor souls were the 'control' group. Their task was to demonstrate and confirm that undergraduate students were also pain adverse. They were strapped into a device that asked them to complete a series of simple number and letter

---

[36] Excuse the pun, I couldn't help myself.
[37] Van Damme S, Van Ryckeghem DM, Wyffels F, Van Hulle L, & Crombez G (2012). No pain no gain? Pursuing a competing goal inhibits avoidance behavior. Pain, 153 (4)

based tasks. The catch was that on completion of 50% of these tasks, the participant received a mildly painful electro-shock.

As you would expect, the group completed very few of these tasks.

The second group were deemed the 'competition' group. This group were provided a slightly different proposition - they were offered a monetary reward. After being strapped into the same device as the control group, this group were provided an incentive. Each time participants in this group were shocked, their input screen showed an increasing point score. The higher the point score, the higher the monetary reward they received.

The result: the second group **willingly** completed far more of the pain-inducing tasks.

If we translate this experiment into our Value Equation, the reason for this result becomes obvious. We end up with a Value Equation that looks something like the following table:

EXPERIMENT GROUP	REWARD	PAIN ENDURED
Control Group (no reward)	- The satisfaction of a completed task.	- A moderately painful electric shock.
Competition Group (reward)	- The satisfaction of a completed task. - A financial reward for each shock-fueled task completed. **PLUS** the researchers unintentionally added gamification elements which created: - A point-based dopamine hit. - The potential for point-based bragging rights among participants and peers.	- A moderately painful electric shock.

Simply put – there was a high task completion rate by the competition group because the Value Equation was balanced back towards the Reward column.

Completing the tasks and enduring the pain became 'worth it'.

STACKING THE EQUATION IN YOUR FAVOUR: A SUSTAINABLE REWARD

This Value Equation is subconsciously at play in all areas of our lives.

It applies to everything we do.

We see a result similar to the Ghent University's zapping experiment when we look at those who stick with exercise habits.

In 2012 a group of academics completed a meta-analysis[38] of the results of exercise motivation studies over the preceding decade. What these researchers found is likely no surprise to you – people are more likely to stick with exercise habits over the long term if they are intrinsically driven rather than extrinsically so.

It's only when we apply the scenario to our Value Equation that the study becomes more illuminating.

Let's look at the case of an extrinsically motivated exerciser. Now, while there are obvious health benefits to exercise, these health benefits are not what are driving this group's decision to do so. After all, if it were – then there wouldn't be the need for extrinsic motivation!

Interestingly, the researchers did find that this group adopted exercise habits in the short term, but that the habits didn't last.

---

[38] Teixeira PJ, Carraça EV, Markland D, Silva MN, Ryan RM. Exercise, physical activity, and self-determination theory: a systematic review. Int J Behav Nutr Phys Act. 2012;9:78. Published 2012 Jun 22.

So, what's really driving this group? And what does their Value Equation look like?

I think we can take a few reasonable guesses here. I'd posit that the exercise habits were put into place by a Value Equation that looks something like the table below.

GROUP	REWARD	PAIN
Extrinsically Motivated Exercisers	- Compliance with a trusted authority. - Avoidance of future conflict or social discomfort.	- Ongoing physical discomfort.

If we assume that this group were given a health and exercise plan by a trusted authority, we see a couple of rewards come into play.

The first is likely a desire to *'do the right thing'.* The right thing in this case is compliance with the advice of a trusted health authority (like a GP).

The second reward is that, by exercising, this group is able to avoid a socially uncomfortable, and perhaps embarrassing scenario at their next 'check-up'.

The combination of these two elements is sufficient enough reward to drive these people to endure the physical discomfort of exercise -> creating a net positive equation.

But, after a short initial boost, these people eventually stop exercising.

So, what happened to that net positive equation?

Well... Decay.

In short – **not all rewards are made equal.**

In this case, the motivational profile of the two rewards that drove the short-term behaviour changed. It decayed. Over time social expectations slip and readjust. Check-in appointments move. Life gets in the way. Once targets start to be missed and the social awkwardness isn't as severe as originally anticipated, then it becomes incredibly easy to rationalise away these rewards.

What's left is a net negative Value Equation.

The story is different for those that are intrinsically motivated.

The research suggests that those that are intrinsically motivated are drawing from an innate desire to satisfy three types of needs:

- Autonomy,
- Competence, and
- Relatedness.

If we translate this into our Value Equation, we end up with something like this:

GROUP	REWARD	PAIN
Intrinsically Motivated Exercisers	- A feeling of autonomy (self-control). - Satisfaction at improving and performing well at a skill. - Positive social feedback and connectedness (for those who exercise with others).	- Ongoing physical discomfort.

It's easy to see how these three rewards create better longevity. Rather than avoiding social awkwardness, this group are creating social connection. Rather than complying with a trusted authority, they are trusting in themselves. These rewards are harder to self-rationalise away. They simply don't decay the way that the extrinsically driven rewards do.

Not All Rewards Are Made Equal

Looking at the longevity of exercise habits gives us a little insight into what makes a strong and sustainable reward column.

We just need to find some form of intrinsic motivation, right?

Oh, if only it were that simple!

Contrary to what popular motivational speakers would have you believe; we cannot expect to harness an intrinsic reward for every process or change we look to roll out. It's a beautiful mirage, but it's just not reality. Everyone has different value sets. Everyone has different contexts.

So, I would suggest your effort is better spent looking at the longevity and natural decay of the rewards you are offering. To demonstrate what I mean, here are a few examples of the different types of motivation patterns that I have observed.

'Volatile' Reward Motivation

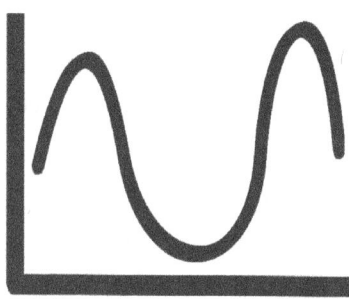

Volatile motivation is typically characterised by large peaks and troughs.

A prime example of where you would see this in the wild is with Audit Compliance activities.

The motivation leading up to and immediately after an Audit is normally high, which then descends to a motivational lull until the next scheduled audit. As that audit nears, motivation rises again and the peak-trough cycle repeats.

'Initial Flash' Reward Motivation

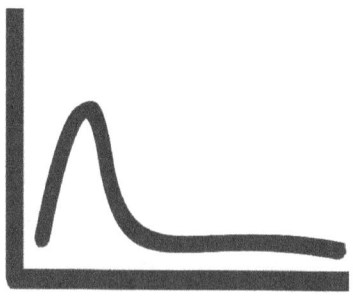

Initial Flash motivation is the 'sugar-hit' of your motivation types. It is typically characterised by a large initial rise then a sharp fall – usually following a key event or milestone.

The motivation levels never typically recover back to the initial levels of excitement. Examples of rewards that generate this type of motivation are:

- A desire to win new funding, with a sharp fall following successful funding allocation.

- A desire to overcome large, noteworthy challenges, with the sharp fall occurring after the challenge is defeated.

- A monetary reward, as while a big monetary influx is initially exciting, it tends to have a sharp motivational decay as an individual adapts to their new 'financial normal'.

'Steady' Reward Motivation

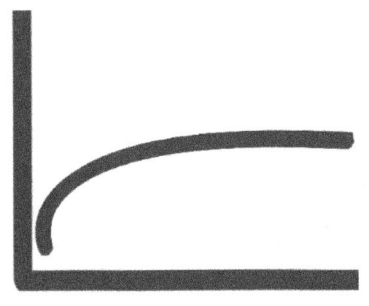

If Initial Flash motivation is your 'sugar hit' then Steady motivation is your 'low GI'. It provides a slow, longer lasting burn.

Thankfully, there are many types of rewards that generate this type of motivation. However, many are contextually conditional. By this I mean they are highly dependent on environmental factors to remain valid.

A few examples of rewards that generate Steady motivation are:

- Something that makes the completion of other tasks dramatically easier.
A reward of this type will be strong only as long as the other tasks that it makes easier are required.

- Something that makes the process of thinking something through easier.

Unlike a notable challenge which is a one-off, a toolset or framework that provides the lubrication for big or challenging thinking will be used again and again.

- Personal satisfaction or success.
  For those that are ambitious, this is an almost endless well of motivation. Note that decay is not the issue with this one, but rather, the difficulty is in finding a way to tap into this ambition. It's often easier said than done.

- Alignment with social customs, organisational culture, or peer standards.
  This is a great way to generate motivation, as it aligns both extrinsic and intrinsic factors (we explore how to generate this in Chapter 5).

- To show off or for personal glory.
  Those that thrive on external validation will have an almost endless well of motivation for this reward. However, the personal glory reward works only for as long as the organisation or the individual's direct management continue to pay attention to the results. A reward of this type can create an inadvertent co-dependency.

There's No Need To Collect Them All

This isn't Pokémon, or a set of Baseball cards. Don't feel you need to collect all of one type of reward or motivation. And please don't feel you need to do a similar motivational sustainability analysis for each of the rewards in your Value Equation.

The truth is that rewards and motivations come in all forms.

The art isn't to only generate rewards with steady motivation – but rather the art is in stacking the deck in your favour. Each reward generates action, just in different amounts.

When you're stacking the reward side of the Value Equation in your favour, keep the nature of the motivational source in mind and don't tie your boat to just one type.

...Now, of course, you could also take advantage of the other way to stack the Value Equation in your favour: reduce their pain.

STACKING THE EQUATION IN YOUR FAVOUR: THE PITA FACTOR

How often have you heard the phrases:

> *'I don't know why we have to do this',* or

> *'I try to avoid dealing with that branch',* or the killer,

> *'They are a total pain in the ass'?*

If you are hearing any of these, then the PITA (Pain In The Ass) Factor is too high.

Your PITA Factor represents the entire right side of the Value Equation, the *'How Painful It Is To Get It'* column. A high PITA score is a solid indicator that others are avoiding what you want done, (or at least trying to!) This is the root of your organisation's shadow processes, non-compliance, and fractured insights.

Thankfully there are only two key sources of pain we need to be looking for.

THE SILENT SOURCE: DISCOMFORT

The first source of pain is Discomfort. Discomfort primarily manifests in either social, mental, or physical forms. Let's break these down.

SOCIAL DISCOMFORT

Social discomfort is when there is a misalignment between an individual and their social environment. This can be either self-driven (e.g., missing the memo stating that the party was formal dress, and you turn up in shorts and T-shirt), or externally driven (e.g., a drunken commuter on a late-night bus making a fool of themself, when everyone else just wants to get home peacefully).

MENTAL DISCOMFORT

Mental discomfort is when there is a mismatch between an individual's mental capability and a task or activity that is assigned to them. Interestingly, this discomfort runs both ways. A genius will feel just as uncomfortable being asked to get the coffees for the room as an apprentice would being asked to manage the build of an entire house. Mental discomfort is about misalignment and imbalance.

PHYSICAL DISCOMFORT

Physical discomfort is the most obvious – it is exactly what it says it is – physical pain. However, it's worth noting that it can take two forms, chronic and acute, both of which have different chances of creating action. A hot pan is often dropped immediately to avoid serious burns, but someone can unintentionally continue past all early indicators of Repetitive Strain Injury (RSI).

In your organisation, it's likely that discomfort underpins more process avoidance and recalcitrance than you think.

Social discomfort is often quietly endured because most staff members have a vested interest in maintaining the status quo. After all, it's the status quo that wins them a paycheck week after week.

Mental discomfort is hidden through other excuses. People often mask inability as change resistance and obstinance.

Physical discomfort is rarely acute, and often chronic. Years of poor posture may be slowly taking a toll on your teams' willingness for risk. After all, risk means change, and who wants to take on change when your back hurts!

The Not-So-Silent Source: Waste

Throughout most of the 20th century, Lean Manufacturing Theory and all its derivatives popularised the idea of waste reduction. During this surge, corporate processes were shrunk and cut to their bare minimums and productivity soared.

...Except, for the many places and processes where it didn't.

Somehow most of the processes in our organisations are still filled with garbage. I won't spend too much time on this as this book isn't a study of Lean theory, however, just in case you haven't ventured into the wide world of Lean – here are the 8 types of Lean waste:

- Defects – delivery of something that fails to meet customer expectations.
- Extra-processing – overengineering something way beyond customer expectations.
- Overproduction – making too much of something.
- Inventory – stockpiling excess things. This is often a byproduct of overproduction.
- Waiting – time spent waiting for something else to occur.
- Underutilised Talent – good people not doing good things.
- Transportation – unnecessarily moving things.
- Motion – unnecessary movement by people and things.

Where this all becomes relevant for our PITA discussion is the emotional pain that waste causes us. We humans seem to have a sixth sense or intuition for process waste. From duplicated forms to excessive wait times. From purposeless meetings to compulsory reports that never get looked at.

Waste creates frustration.

Just walk into your local car licensing centre and watch the people there. Some degree of a wait is generally accepted but watch what happens when the wait time grows longer.

You would see frustration build in people's body language.

First, people may start by tapping their feet or hands.

Then they may escalate to long looks at staff members to indicate displeasure, and perhaps a silent cry for help.

Then may come the long, audible, obvious sighs. Or moving about just a little too loudly.

Finally, they may approach a staff member to enquire about the wait time.

Eventually, after enough time has passed, the pain of the wait will be so acute that it will overwhelm any potential reward of achieving their objective. Even to the point of overwhelming the sunk cost of the time already spent there. At that point, you would see that person walk out (usually fuming).

Waste is no small fry. Mismanagement of waste will make or break your change efforts.

The great thing about waste-driven-frustration is that, unlike discomfort, which is usually silent, frustration is often verbally expressed. This means it is easier to pinpoint and identify. Just look for the public declarations of exasperation! (Of course, it's better to find the waste before that point.)

THE INSIDIOUS SOURCE OF CHANGE WASTE – EGO

"If there's anything more important than my ego around, I want it caught and shot now.

- The Hitchhikers Guide To The Galaxy, Douglas Adams

While we are talking about painful waste, let's take a moment to talk about something that simultaneously drives people crazy, while bloating out too many projects and programs.

Ego.

HOW EGO STOPPED A SPACESHIP

In the late 20-teens, Spaceship Capital was the 'up and coming' investment fund to watch. It was meant to shake up the Australian superannuation[39] industry; targeting tech-savvy younger workers with its one core belief: *Invest where the world is going*. Since 2016 it had enlisted customers into its new super fund with the promise of targeting investment into fast growing tech companies domestically and across the world.

And it was working.

The company was growing at a substantial rate, with over 40,000 new clients in just the 2018 Financial Year.

---

[39] Superannuation is a compulsory scheme in Australia where a person has money paid by their employer to a super fund so they are financially supported when they retire from the workforce.

The thing was, Spaceship was still yearning to 'grow-up'. In its current form, it was only acting as a 'promoter' for another fund - Tidswell Financial Services. The idea was that it would start as a promoter, then make the move out from under the Tidswell umbrella to become a standalone investment firm.

That was until April 2019, when it was announced that Spaceship had withdrawn its application for a Registrable Superannuation Entity (RSE) licence - the very thing it needed to run its own tech-focused super funds.

And what was the issue with their RSE application? Their CEO/co-founder Paul Bennetts had too centralised a role and too much formalised control over their customers' results.

In trying to create his vision, this CEO ultimately blocked his own progress. It's also likely no coincidence that Paul Bennetts was the only original co-founder left from Spaceship's starting four.

Seems that ego strikes again.

The Ego Component

Spaceship's predicament reminds me of a conversation with a friend. He and his company had been developing a piece of software for the last 18 months. It had been a long, hard slog, but the end was in sight.

I felt for my friend. I was vicariously both excited and exhausted for him... That was until he told me something that absolutely blew my mind.

> *"Yeah, most of what is left I am doing for me, the customer result will largely be the same".*

And that's the thing here. Both Paul Bennetts from Spaceship and my (intentionally unnamed) friend have a vision they are pursuing. But both are, against their own interests, adding additional time and cost to the end result.

This is **'The Ego Component'**: The elements of the change kept in because the change leader wants them, and not because they add any value to the customers of the end vision.

And for everyone other than the change leader – this is a VERY painful source of waste.

The humorous thing here is that counter-intuitively – **our visions are best realised when we think not of what we achieve, but what we can now help others achieve.**

In other words – not adding things just because we want them.

Deploying The Value Equation In Your Change

I've read so many books with mindset chapters that are just filled with useless aspirational thinking. You probably have too. Books filled with aphorisms like:

"Nothing is impossible."

"Colonel Sanders (of KFC fame) was rejected over 1000 times."

"Happiness depends on your mindset, and attitude."

Thankfully, this isn't one of those books.

So, here's the 5 key steps to ensure you're driving a positive result in your Value Equation.

1) Identify the people you want to change.
2) Consider their reward for changing.
3) Consider the pain they will need to endure to get the reward.
4) Halve the weight you are mentally placing on the reward items and double the weight of the pain side.
5) Then run the equation by a representative or three from the impacted group(s).

If the consensus is that yes, that will be valuable, then you should be in the clear.

But what if it's not?

Well, then you have 4 options:

1) Do it anyway, and deal with the poor results.
2) Don't do it and stick with the status quo.
3) Find a way to increase the reward side of the equation.
4) Find a way to decrease the pain side of the equation.

Now I'm sure you can see the flaws with Option 1, that is, forcing your people to 'do it anyway'. But I won't lie here, there are times and places where Option 1 is what's needed. The ol' 'captains call' remains a useful part of leadership, but it can't be your go-to option and must be used selectively.

Option 2 on the other hand is interesting. It threatens the initial WHY of your change, but should raise valid questions – like:

"Why are we doing this, if the value doesn't stack up?"

Or we look at options 3 and 4. Increasing reward and decreasing pain.

Throughout the rest of this book, we cover a number of different strategies you can put in place to both increase reward and decrease pain. But for those of you who can't wait, here's one that's rather brilliant.

Gamification:
The Art of Creating New Rewards

On May 25th, 2018, the World Health Organisation (WHO) added "gaming disorder" as a behavioral addiction to the International Classification of Diseases. This was a controversial move and one that echoed throughout the gaming industry for a few months.

But for anyone who's taken public transport, this probably wasn't a surprise for you. Catch any bus or train at peak time and you'll see that 95% of people are on their phones. Sneak a peek at what they are doing on said phone – and half of the time it'll be a game of some sort.

First there was Angry Birds, the iPhone game that was so successful that a production studio spent over $73 million USD to turn it into a movie. Then there was Flappy Bird, the game that created wealth for Dong Nguyen, a Vietnamese programmer, at a pace that would make Mark Zuckerberg envious. The wealth and fame grew so fast that it scared Dong off and he pulled the game down. Then for a while it was Candy Crush, which at its peak in 2014 was pulling over $1 Million USD a day. Not bad for a game that was free to download. Now it's likely something else.

Thankfully all these commuters aren't dealing with WHO-diagnosed gaming disorder, as when the train or bus pulls up, they are able to put the phone away, get up and disembark.

But there's no denying it. Gaming is big business. In fact, estimates for 2020 put the worldwide video game industry at $179

Billion USD. That's larger than the global film and American sports industries combined.[40]

Clearly, we humans like our games.

And this doesn't just apply to video games.

Let's briefly revisit the Ghent University pain avoidance experiment that we covered earlier in this chapter. Take another look at the table below. Without meaning to, the researchers added 2 gamification rewards for the Competition Group – further stacking their reward column.

EXPERIMENT GROUP	REWARD	PAIN ENDURED
Competition Group (reward)	- The satisfaction of a completed task. - A financial reward for each shock-fueled task completed. **PLUS** the researchers unintentionally added gamification elements which created: - A point-based dopamine hit. - The potential for point-based bragging rights among participants peers.	- A moderately painful electric shock

---

[40] 179.7 Billion USD in Video games, compared to $100 Billion USD in global film and $75 Billion USD in North American sports. *https://www.marketwatch.com/story/videogames-are-a-bigger-industry-than-sports-and-movies-combined-thanks-to-the-pandemic-11608654990*

First was the dopamine hit that we all get when seeing our scores go up. Whether you grew up playing Pinball, Pong or Call of Duty – you likely know how good racking up a top personal score feels.

Second, these researchers added a points-based opportunity for score comparison and peer bragging. Anyone who has ever played laser tag knows this reward all too well.

If the researchers had added a progression mechanic, like 'levelling up' based on either speed or pain tolerance, then I suspect task completion would have been even higher.

Gamification is a powerful strategy for increasing the rewards offered in your Value Equation. But this idea of gamification isn't new. Many organisations use gamification in one way or another.

Some do it well.

Others don't.

But What Even Is Gamification?

To figure out how we can best use gamification to bolster the reward side of our Value Equations, we must first stop and take a good look at what gamification is. In a fantastic paper[41] from the Kelley School of Business in Indiana, USA, we learn that gamification is the:

---

[41] Robson K, Kietzmann J, Plangger K, McCarthy I P, (2015). Is it all a game? Understanding the principles of gamification.

> *"Application of game design principles in non-gaming contexts".*

In other words, gamification is taking the key elements that make games rewarding and leveraging those elements to drive improved results in our organisations.

The thing is, this is by no means a new idea. A study by Gartner in 2011 suggested that 70% of the world's largest public companies would be using gamified application by 2013. For a time there, it seemed that gamification would be the 'one ring to rule them all' when it came to employee and customer motivation.

Except that didn't happen.

So, what went wrong? Why didn't gamification take off over the last decade?

Simply put – the games were boring.

Gamification fell prey to the buzzword trap. Organisations everywhere started shoehorning games into everything. Did a game even make sense? Would it even drive the emotional feedback loop they are after? Who cares! Gamify all the things!

So yeah.

That didn't work.

But that doesn't mean gamification doesn't. It does, but it needs to be designed and used appropriately.

Let's take a moment to explore what makes up a game. Drawing on the Kelley Business School paper again, we get a nice clear model.

The Elements of a Game

In essence a game has 3 parts:

1. **Mechanics** – the gaming context. This includes the rules, goals, setting, interactions, and boundaries. These are known before the experience starts and remain constant throughout the game.
2. **Dynamics** – the types of player behaviours that emerge as they play the game. These are produced by how the players follow the mechanics of the game. For example, it could be cheating or bluffing as in Poker, or conspiring like in Monopoly, touching gloves before an MMA fight, or the various forms of good and poor sportsmanship in cricket, football, or your sport of choice.
3. **Emotions** – the mental reactions that players feel while playing. For a game to be effective there must be some sort of positive emotion reinforcement loop. Examples here include the dopamine boost of hitting a high score, or the adrenaline rush of a last-minute clutch victory.

So, to return to the question at hand. Why do most organisations fall flat with their gamification efforts?

They only consider the mechanics!

Good gamification is like sex. The mechanics is the boring part. It must be more than mechanics. It must engage our mind and emotions.

Further, most organisations ignore the four role types necessary for a true gamified experience. When most people think of a game, they only think of the player, but there's more than that. Each role is crucial for the game's reinforcement loops, and ultimately each role is crucial for a game's success.

The four roles are:

1) The **Designers** – those that make decisions about the mechanics of the game.
2) The **Players** – those that compete directly in the game.
3) The **Spectators** - those that view, monitor, and interact with a game without actively playing. Spectators are responsible for generating a game's atmosphere.
4) The **Observers** – those that are passively aware of and involved in the experience, but with no direct impact on the game. However, it's often this group that dictates the 'stakes' of the game. The more observers, the greater the pressure on the players.

With the full model now in mind, take a moment and think about an instance of gamification that you have experienced in the past.

Was there purposeful design of all 3 elements (mechanics, dynamics, and emotions)? Or was it purely focused on the mechanics?

What about its roles? Was it player-centric, or was it actively aware of each of the four roles?

To provide you something to contrast with – let's take a quick look at one of the most successful gamified processes of all time: Pop Idol.

POP IDOL – A GAMIFIED MASTERPIECE

If you haven't been living under a rock for the last few decades, then you're probably aware of the TV series *Pop Idol* (and its global derivatives, American Idol in the US, Australian Idol here in Aus., and 43 others across the globe).

> *"But Brendon,"*

You may say,

> *"Pop Idol isn't a gamified process, it's a gameshow!"*

And I'll be honest with you here, I initially thought that too. That was until I dug a little deeper.

Are you ready to have your mind blown?

Consider with me for a moment the traditional method of finding talent to sign to a record label. A record label relies on a series of individual talent scouts, who each have a 'scene', specialisation, or region they cover. The actual work of scouting is labour-intensive and has a high failure rate. Not to mention the audience engagement for these newly signed artists is usually time-limited and geographically localised.

Records are primarily sold by running billboard chart style lists every week, driving arbitrary rankings of the 'newest hits'.

That was all until Simon Fuller flipped the format.

Is your mind connecting the dots yet?

Simon Fuller did to talent scouting what 'free offerings on the internet' did to marketing. He made their clients come to them. Except he one-upped it. He made it an entertaining game. And with a lifetime revenue of over $2.5 Billion USD, what a game it was!

The mechanics were simple. Players (contestants) would audition each week, hoping to survive a broader knock-out style competitive structure driven by spectator (audience) voting. The dynamics were exciting – with competition, scandals and humour. The emotions were intense, driving spectator and observer fanaticism similar to that of a local sports team. And player emotions shifting from hope to glee to exhaustion to aspiration to jealously to stress to, ultimately, the pleasure of victory or the crush of defeat.

There's no denying it. Pop Idol was an outstanding success in gamifying industry processes.

GAMIFYING ON A SMALLER SCALE

Now, unfortunately, we don't all have huge production budgets to make multi-billion-dollar franchises. But the elements and roles stay the same. It's just a matter of scale.

Your game (probably) won't be a global sensation, but there's no reason it can't be a local one.

Here's the questions to ask (and answer) to drive effective gamification into your change and boost your Value Equations.

1) Who will perform each role, and how will interactions be enabled?
2) WIIFT (What's In It For Them) – why would someone play? Why would someone watch or even care about the results of the game?
3) What are the rewards you are looking to drive into your Value Equation?
4) What's the goal of the game? (try to keep it to one.)
5) How could the game be broken, and does it matter if it is?
6) How will the game adapt, and what game-parts shouldn't change?
7) What's the end game? When and how will the game end?

But here's the thing.

Gamification is by no means a panacea for bad engagement. What it is though is an effective way to boost the reward column of your Value Equations and drive additional motivation. Which, for Value Equations that are feeling a little too 'neutral' in their result, can be the difference between success and failure.

A Final Note On A Valuable Mindset

Like the Ghent University researchers found, the accepted industry standard for driving a new or changed behaviour is also noticeably one-sided. However, while the researcher's focus was on Pain, the change industry is obsessed with Reward.

Ever heard of WIIFM?

WIIFM (What's In It For Me) is the go-to approach to driving change outcomes. But, as you've seen, that's only half of the equation. **It doesn't matter what's in it for them if it's too painful to get!**

Overt or not, the Value Equation underpins the success of any change that requires someone, somewhere, to do something differently. Given that 95% of your organisational change initiatives meet that definition – it's worth paying attention to.

VALUABLE CHANGE

Chapter 5: Rally Your People

"Momentum solves 80% of your problems

- John C. Maxwell

Out of all the ideas we have discussed so far, this may well be the most self-evident.

You can't create change without your people.

And yet stakeholder profiling and communication planning are some of the most ignored documents across most change initiatives. Our obsession with the 'WHAT' of the change not only clouds our view of the WHY[42], but also the Who!

Unfortunately, like the complex spiderweb charts that attempt to explain a change's WHY – the industry has also overcomplicated the 'Who' question. Stakeholder profiles, engagement strategies, communication approaches, impact assessments, change readiness questionnaires, saturation heatmaps and many more. Despite their often useful content, the truth is that when it comes

---

[42] As we covered in chapter 1.

to engaging and working with the people component of our changes – it's all too easy to fall into document overwhelm.

When there are too many documents, it just becomes too hard.

So, rather than picking and choosing the ones to best suit their needs, the whole document set regularly gets ignored.

What is missing is a coherent framework, not just a list of documents, but rather an approach that focuses on all of the people involved in the change. The framework must include not only how to best engage and work with people across your organisation, but also how maximise both your own team(s) momentum and your change's organisational reach. After all, what use is a stakeholder impact analysis if your own team is flat, morale is low, and turnover is high? And what use is a communications strategy if you are targeting (almost) aimlessly across your organisation?

...Naturally, this is where I let you know that there's a better, more effective way.

The Better, More Effective Way: The VP Approach

It's time to introduce you to one of the most cohesive people approaches out there. And, true to form, I've kept it ridiculously simple for you.

It's the Valuable People (VP) Approach, and it has just 3 elements.

1. Build and Protect Core Momentum.
2. Identify and Enlist Internal Influencers.
3. Engage & Grow through Community.

Which, when put together, looks a little like the below:

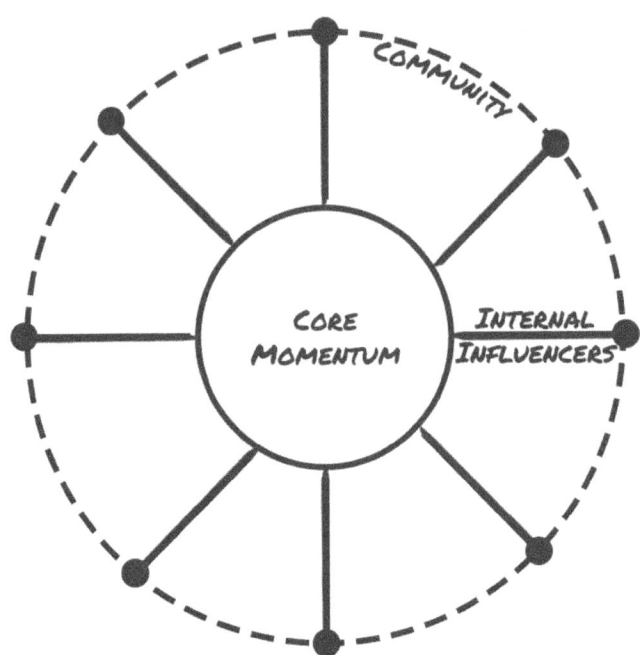

The VP Approach is designed to care for and rally everyone involved in your project, both inside and out. The order of its elements is also very intentional.

First, you must start with your core people, and who is more core to your project than your project team(s)! As the controversial Jordan Peterson says,

> "If you can't even clean up your own room, who the hell are you to give advice to the world?"

This should **always** be the first place to start for any change success.

For those of you that are skeptical of this claim, I want you to do a little mental exercise with me. Think back to the last time you attended a nice restaurant.

How were the wait staff?

Friendly?

Rude?

Exhausted?

Exuberant?

Sassy?

Now reflect for a moment. How much did that staff member's own emotional position influence your experience?

In all but the few cases that prove the rule[43], a flat, unenthusiastic, or rude staff member will tarnish your restaurant experience.

The same is true in our change initiatives. If our team(s) are flat, cynical or filled with despair and fear, then our target stakeholders will be too. On the other hand, if your change team(s) are tackling each day with a high motivational intensity, then that too will be contagious. But there's a level even better than that. What if your change team(s) were willing to organically declare and share the great things that you are doing across the organisation? The results of that are always nothing short of amazing.

So that's where you start, with your core people.

Once you have generated and garrisoned the momentum of your team(s), you can turn your eye outward. It's time to find your champions – those people that will hold the banner for your change inside your target stakeholder groups. The issue is, how do you find these people? Well, there are currently two approaches that are commonly used here:

Either,

a) you ask for volunteers, or
b) you pick your pet favourites.

The bad news is that both options are terrible ways to go about it. Thankfully, recent developments in the field of network science

---

[43] The exception here is Dick's Last Resort, a bar and restaurant chain in the United States known for its intentional employment of obnoxious staff. Patrons of Dick's expect to be insulted or placed in socially uncomfortable situations as part of their dining experience.

have given us a better way – and in a turn of events that shouldn't be a surprise to you now – it's all about asking the right questions.

In fact, with just 2 questions you will find the scientifically backed influencers throughout your stakeholder groups. Finding and enlisting these influencers massively decreases the effort needed to communicate, inform, and engage with your stakeholder groups. It also increases the likelihood of change success by leveraging the established reputations of these organisational influencers.

Finally, the third element of the VP Approach is to Engage and Grow through Community. With your influencers at the helm, it's then time to widen your outward reach through the creation of communities. The problem is - most organisational communities suck. Boring and self-serving, they often fail in just a few months.

Let's avoid doing that. In the next chapter I'll show you how. But let's not get ahead of ourselves here. Let's start at the first element: Build and Protect Core Momentum.

So, without further ado, let's dive in!

BUILD AND PROTECT CORE MOMENTUM: ELEVATING FROM DESPAIR TO FANATICISM

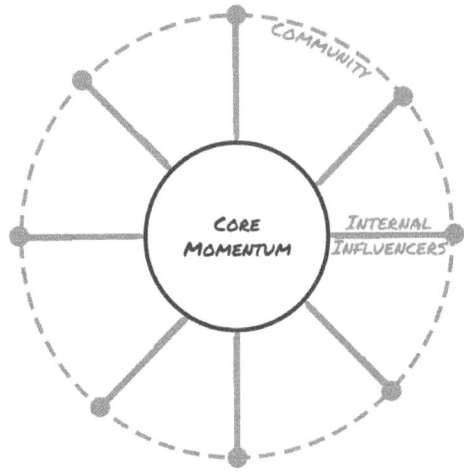

There's a concerning trend that I've seen across too many change delivery efforts. Sooner or later, the staff within these initiatives grow worn, cynical and lifeless.

It's usually a combination of change resistance and revolving door executive sponsorship that absolutely destroys change momentum and morale, but it can be other things too. Often the staff can intuitively see the writing on the wall, but are sticking around because, hey, at least it's a pay cheque.

However, even if your change teams aren't stuck in the depths of despair, not enough staff are willing to stand at the top of a building and shout glory for their change! (...or at least talk up the cool things that their change initiative is doing).

So, no matter where you and your team(s) are, there is probably room for growth. Therefore, I'd like to introduce you to the Momentum Path (shown below). The Momentum Path enables you to diagnose the current momentum level of each member of your team[44], and then provides you a clear strategy on what to put in place to promote continued growth.

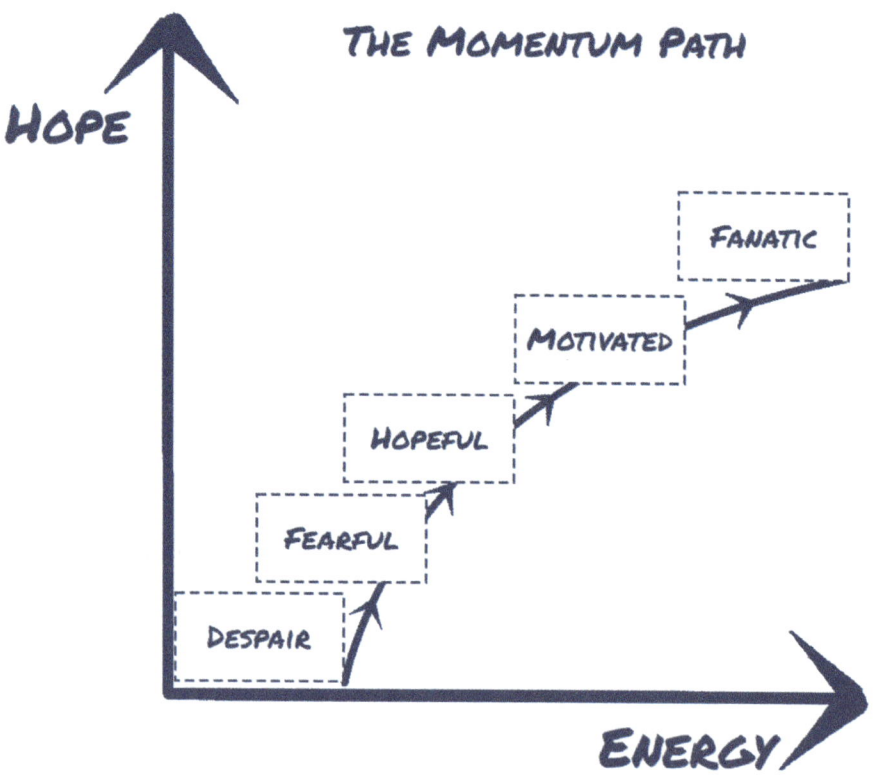

---

[44] Yourself included.

When considering momentum, you must look at two key elements – Hope and Energy.

For clarity here, I'm not talking about energy in a pseudo-science sense, or even an electrical one. I'm using the term energy closer to the way that one could describe a 4-year-old child, that is *'Full of Energy'*. Energy is a sense of attentiveness, enthusiasm, and urgency.

Hope, on the other hand can be thought of as a blend of the belief in the validity and usefulness of the work being done and an optimism for their personal future as part of this work.

I've found that the higher the energy and hope within your team, the higher the momentum. It makes sense then, that these two elements form the x and y axes for The Momentum Path. Plotted within you will find 5 levels:

- Despair,
- Fearful,
- Hopeful,
- Motivated, and
- Fanatic.

These 5 levels cover the breadth of momentum types that you will work with as you build momentum and morale within your change team(s).

To put this into context for you, a team at its lowest point – Despair, has no interest in their work. They will be producing low to no useful output and will have no vacation or sick days left (as the days are taken as soon as they are available).

On the other hand, a team at its highest point - Fanatic will be eagerly engaging in each conversation, thriving with excitement to share new ideas. They will be talking about your change initiative with friends and family. Teams with high momentum love coming to work, and truly believe in what they are doing.

Clearly, we want less Despair and more Fanaticism.

IDENTIFYING WHERE YOU (AND YOUR TEAM) ARE

Organisational energy is intangible – the measurement of which is not as simple as looking at a balance sheet (although sometimes there are some clues there). There is also a temptation to use qualitative measurements to gauge the levels of energy and hope by running surveys, focus groups, and the like. However, I've found that one of the most effective methods of gauging organisational energy is simply *observing*.

Momentum is felt rather than seen.

So, my advice here is trust your gut. If you've been working with your team for longer than a few weeks, then you will have picked up enough of a sense of the culture to be able to make a judgement.

But, for those who prefer a more analytical approach, feel free to release your inner Sherlock Holmes and look for clues in:

- The level of absenteeism,
- Time spent on non-work activity (e.g., surfing the internet),
- The general 'buzz' and franticness of your team – or a lack thereof,
- Regular high or low moods,
- An inability to deal with stress,
- High or low change resistance, or
- Change fatigue and exhaustion.

Strategies To Level Up

What's interesting with the Momentum Path is that the strategy for one level is different to the strategy for another.

In other words, as Marshall Goldsmith says :

> "What got you here, won't get you there".

Let's spend some time together and explore each level of the path, and what's needed to level up your momentum.

A quick note here before we dive into the specifics for each level. You may have noticed in the earlier diagram that the first few levels almost seem to vertically stack on top of each other, then the last few spread out wide to the right. This is to reflect a crucial point.

Hope precedes Energy.

First, we must find ways to create Hope. Then, and only then, can we look to generate energy.

FROM DESPAIR TO FEARFUL

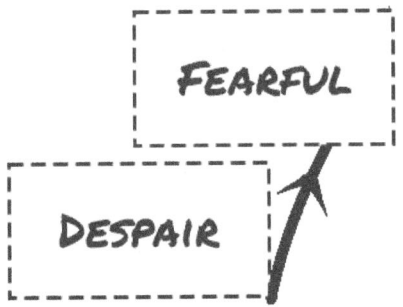

Those in Despair suffer from a complete and utter lack of hope. These people despise coming into work every day and are very likely miserable. They almost always feel stuck, because if they didn't, you can be sure they would have moved on already.

A primary factor for those in Despair is a feeling that their work at your organisation doesn't matter. They have given up and will just do the bare minimum to get by.

Teams stuck in Despair are some of the most difficult to work with, and as much as we would all love to pretend that they don't exist – we've all come into direct contact with them throughout our careers (or perhaps have been there ourselves!).

Key Strategies for Those in Despair

Provide An Excuse For Hope

There's a key issue at play with those stuck in Despair – and that is that they are stuck!

The thing is, we humans don't like to be wrong. What this means is that very rarely will we willingly change our minds without some form of new information or decision catalyst. This is especially so with strongly held negative views.

So, to break the shackles of Despair, your aim here is to discretely **give those in Despair the permission to change their mind.** None of us want to feel we are inconsistent, so there needs to be a notable change in something around them.

In short - they need an excuse to change their mind.

This requires a physical change in either one or more of the following:

- Who (their team),
- What (their work),
- When (their timetabling),
- Where (their location), or
- How (their systems and processes).

It's important to keep in mind that these changes will be met with absolute cynicism by those in Despair. The flicker of hope may not be obvious, but it will be there. And both you and they need it.

FROM FEARFUL TO HOPEFUL

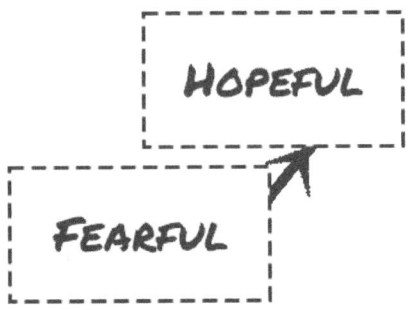

Those in Fearful have just a small seed of hope – they wish for more but are characterised by a disproportionate level of fear and skepticism.

Often fueled by previous experiences where they were left behind, embarrassed, or not considered – the work output from this group is also low, usually still only the bare minimum.

An extremely common theme for those in the fearful position is again a feeling that the work they do adds no real value to the organisation. However, unlike those in Despair, the Fearful haven't given up. Instead, they may well have good ideas but avoid instigating any change in case it places their position at risk.

An effective element of working with those stuck in the Fearful stage is to identify the source of their fear. So, let's take a brief detour to look at the 7 most common fears (which I term the *'The Deadly 7'.*)

THE DEADLY 7

'The Deadly 7' - it sounds like a league of super-villains.

> *"Ah, you may have foiled us today Batman, but the Deadly 7 will get you next time!"*

Thankfully, this group of 7 don't wield super-powers. Their power instead comes from their insidious ability to stifle innovation, lower work engagement and diminish productivity.

The Deadly 7 are also scarily commonplace. As we work through each of the fears, take a moment to reflect on whether you have seen that fear play out in your career; either felt directly yourself, or vicariously through a colleague. I suspect that you will have seen most, if not all, of these fears at play. Let's briefly explore each one.

1. A FEAR OF BEING CUT DOWN (TALL POPPY)

Our first fear is one that is particularly prevalent in my home country of Australia: Tall Poppy Syndrome.

Supposedly coined sometime in 1864, 'Tall Poppy Syndrome' is the levelling derision of anyone who thinks they should stand higher than everyone else. There are many claims to its origins, but I suspect that its roots in Australian culture formed as a rejection of the class structure inherited from our English heritage.

Tall Poppy is a great equaliser but suffers a major issue. More often than not, cultures that embrace a Tall Poppy mentality end up cutting down any person who seeks to be a standout success.

The net result of a team or individual suffering from this fear is an aversion to risk, not because they are afraid of the risk going wrong – but rather they are afraid of the risk going right!

No risk taking = stifled innovation, lower engagement, and diminished productivity.

2. A Fear of Meaningless Work

Anyone that has worked in a large, bureaucratic organisation likely knows the feeling all too well.

It's late on a Friday afternoon. You start packing your bag when a last-minute work request comes in. You sit back down, unpack, and start pulling it together. You even cash in some favours with your colleagues to get it done.

…Time passes, and you miss your social plans. But that's OK because this work was urgently needed.

Finally, you complete your review, attach the document, and send the email. With a sigh of relief, you again pack your bags and enjoy your well earned weekend – only to come in on Monday and find out that:

> *"That last minute report? Oh, that was bumped from the agenda."*

No one even looked at it.

Yet another piece of work that will sit in a digital file, gathering digital dust. Never to be seen or used again.

It's a story that I've both lived and witnessed too many times.

This fear creates two major issues. The first, and most obvious – there is a notable amount of wasted work effort. Work effort that could be spent on other, more useful things. I do a lot of work with public sector organisations, and this is a huge problem in all of them. I haven't run the numbers, but I wouldn't be surprised if hundreds of thousands of staff hours are burned each year on examples just like the one above. [45]

However, it's the second issue that is more insidious. Experiences like the one above creates organisational cynics. The cynicism is a mechanism to hide the underlying fear – a fear of caring enough about something to put in the work, only for it to end up meaningless. This protective cynicism isn't healthy. It's not selectively applied, and its often directed towards all work indiscriminately as it can be hard to tell ahead of time which bit of work will be ignored.

The net result again is an aversion to risk, stifled innovation, lower engagement, and diminished productivity.

3. A Fear of Insufficient Skill

Like the fears that came before it, a fear of insufficient skill is often masked by other protective personas, the most common being cynicism or a *'holier than thou'* approach. The individual

---

[45] Which is yet another reason why using Simplest Practical, Question-oriented artefacts are so important, like we discussed in Chapter 3.

experiencing this fear often deploys distractions to divert attention from their own ability, or lack thereof.

The essence of the fear is simple – it's a fear of not being skilled enough to succeed. If an individual doesn't feel they are *'good enough'* then that individual won't expose themselves to a risk of failure.

Again, this fear creates a risk aversion, stifling innovation and lowering work engagement.

4. A Fear of Being Taken Advantage Of

Interestingly, the opposite to insufficient skill is also a catalyst for a fear – a fear of being taken advantage of. Anyone who is high in skill but low in assertiveness is particularly at risk here.

This fear is epitomised by the character 'Milton' from the 1999 cult-hit film Officespace. For those that haven't seen the film – Milton has an inability to firmly say 'No'. Unfortunately, this means he ends up without his favourite stapler and moved to a desk hidden down in the depths of the basement. Thankfully, Milton is an extreme case, but like all good comedy, Officespace draws its inspirations from reality. When someone is scared of being taken advantage of, they will often hide their talent, doing just enough to get by. Or, if their talent becomes known, they will work begrudgingly, lowering both productivity and innovation.

5. A Fear of Breaking Norms

This fear is firmly rooted in your organisational culture. In short, your cultural status quo is a worthy adversary for any innovative mind. If the status quo is one that is risk adverse, or one that doesn't promote honest and open discussion, then your team(s) are unlikely to challenge ideas or overtly drive improvement for fear of being labelled the *'weird one'*.

6. A Fear of Embarrassment

A rather self-explanatory fear – a fear of embarrassment is a natural result of a lack of skill, poor cultural fit, or an over-active feeling of imposter syndrome[46].

No one likes being embarrassed, so they will avoid situations that place them at risk of being so.

7. A Fear of Personal Non-Alignment

This fear is a little different from the previous 6 and seems to be a more modern phenomenon. With the expansion of motivational speakers, personal coaches and an endless stream of aspirational content delivered to us through the internet – there is an increasing desire to *'do something fulfilling'*. While this is a valiant goal for us all to seek, unfortunately for many, doing something fulfilling is rooted firmly in fantasy – all the good bits with none of the work.

This shift in desire has introduced a new fear into our workplaces – a fear of personal non-alignment. Simply put, a fear of personal non-alignment is when someone holds themselves back from

---

[46] Imposter syndrome is loosely defined as doubting your abilities and feeling like a fraud. It disproportionately affects high-achieving people, who find it difficult to accept their accomplishments. Many question whether they're deserving of accolades. – HBR.org

giving any more than, say, 60% of their effort into their work because they are concerned that it's *'not one of their passions'.*

There are three key drivers underlying this fear:

1. A desire to avoid living a sub-standard life (against a glamourous but unrealistic social media benchmark).
2. A desire to live one's passions, but without any clear idea of what those passions actually are, and
3. A worry that one may well be genuinely talented at *'boring work'...* if one is good at boring work, then does that mean that they themselves are boring?

Interestingly, despite its recent origins, the end result of this fear is again a lack of engagement, risk aversion and stifled innovation. After all, who wants to put extra effort into something that isn't *'speaking to them personally'?*

KEY STRATEGIES FOR THOSE IN FEARFUL

So, with this understanding of the Deadly 7, how do we counter this and pull our people from Fearful to Hopeful?

Well, to create hope in this group we must attack on two fronts.

NORMALISE SUCCESS, FAILURE AND REFLECTION

First, we must normalise success, failure, and reflection. I outlined my suggestions on how to do this as part of the Learning Habit Driver's Aid in Chapter 3 of this book. This normalisation tackles 3 of the key fears of the Deadly 7: Tall Poppy, Trespassing Norms and Embarrassment.

CREATE A CHALLENGE PATH

Second, we must help our team(s) generate meaningful traction. The best way to do this is to utilise a challenge path.

Start your team(s) with work that is low challenge but high to medium value. Then, once that work is conquered, move your team(s) to the next piece of work, with each progression increasing in difficulty. All work must have a clear linkage to organisational and change success. You are aiming to build up the belief that they belong where they are. This actively counters the fears of Meaningless Work, Insufficient Skill, Being Taken Advantage of and Personal Non-Alignment.

Creating a challenge path is easy, and only takes a few steps.

1. Set a short-term vision (no more than a month),
2. Run a challenge path design session by:
   a. Listing the challenges/activities required to hit the vision.
   b. Capturing the respective size and impact of these challenges.
   c. Reordering for the lowest size and largest impact.
   d. Setting ownership and commitment.
3. Conquer,
4. Reflect.

From Hopeful to Motivated

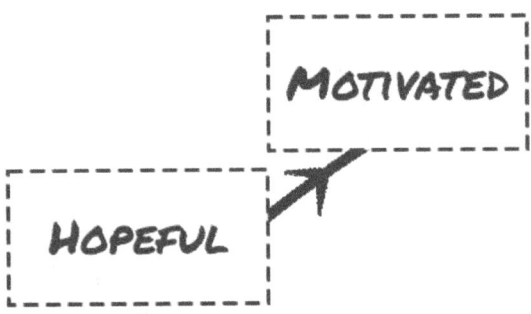

Those in Hopeful want to do good for the organisation but are risk-adverse. While they are not debilitated by fear, they are still unsure of either their fit, contribution or skillset.

Most new staff start here.

Key Strategies for Those in Hopeful

We are now transitioning from those that are skeptical of the organisation (Despair and Fearful) to those that are neutral and open. What this means for our strategies is that we are switching from a path of overcoming fears and baggage to one of generating motivation.

Motivation is built on three key paths – challenge, empowerment, and clear contribution[47]. Accordingly, there are 3 key strategies here.

REAL CHALLENGE & GAMIFICATION

While we provided low challenge, high contribution opportunities for those in Fearful, those in Hopeful want to prove 'they can do it'. They need dragons to slay[48]. This means that they need an escalating set of challenges. Conquering one encourages progress to the next. Gamification strategies like 'levelling up' and tiered rewards can be useful to pursue and implement here. Try to create mechanisms for sharing and recognition among peers. This encourages ownership and will produce new ideas for your change efforts. We covered gamification in more detail in Chapter 4.

EMPOWERMENT

We must provide those that are hopeful with the opportunity to self-select. What this means is that, while we may provide a path of increasing challenge, the Hopeful must be able to select and have input into what the next challenge will be. Two-way trust is essential here.

---

[47] Which of course echoes the great work in Daniel Pink's 'Drive: The Surprising Truth About What Motivates Us'.
[48] Or domesticate, if 'How To Train Your Dragon' is more their style...

Clear Contribution

We must protect those that are hopeful against any backward slide that could be caused by meaningless work. It's crucial that your team(s)' work has real meaning for the organisation and the change initiative's forward movement. In other words, there must be a clearly visible path through the following.

Organisational Strategy ->

    Strategic Plan ->

        Personal Plan ->

            Personal Results ->

                Organisational Results

From Motivated to Fanatic

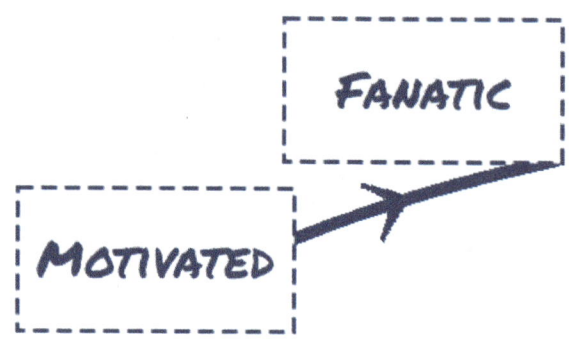

Those in Motivated are fantastic contributors for your change and organisation more broadly. They are highly reliable, self-driven members of staff who take action to ensure a good result for both themselves and your organisation.

There is, however, one step higher – 'Fanatic'.

Fanatics don't just like coming to work – **they love it.** Their obsessions drive them. They actively self-label as being a part of your organisation, not just working for it. They advocate internally for you with any staff that are at lower momentum levels, and are beacons of light within your area, groups, and teams.

Key Strategies for Those in Motivated

Building Fanatics is difficult. Don't get me wrong though, it is absolutely worth it. True fanaticism can be strong enough to overcome almost any sort of pain. After all, we all know the story of the Apple fanatics who lined up days in advance just to get the newest iPhone. Or the Potterheads: those Harry Potter fans that would dress up in costume and stand in line for midnight book releases as a sign of their true dedication (minting the author J.K. Rowling over a billion dollars in the process).

So, what's behind this fanaticism?

Well, two key things:

1) A strong sense of belonging, and
2) Operating beyond expectation.

And while building these into your change teams may not buy you a castle as it did Ms. Rowling, it will make your life dramatically easier by reducing friction within your team(s) and accelerating uptake across your target stakeholders.

STRATEGIC BELONGING

Belonging was a key tenet of Brené Brown's best seller: 'Braving the Wilderness'. To quote her,

> "True belonging is not passive. It's not the belonging that comes with just joining a group. It's not fitting in or pretending or selling out because it's safer. It's a practice that requires us to be vulnerable, get uncomfortable, and learn how to be present with people without sacrificing who we are. We want true belonging, but it takes tremendous courage to knowingly walk into hard moments."

The question for us then is how can we help our teams feel that sense of belonging? I've found that the strategic use of three tactics here goes a long way towards this:

ENSURE THE SPACE IS SAFE.

We talked about normalising success, failure, and reflection earlier in this chapter. Build on that with good hearted humour and a person-first approach and you've got yourself a recipe for openness and safety.

BUILD A SHARED, ASPIRATIONAL VISION.

A lack of clarity is one of the main killers of workforce motivation. Ensure that a clear, aspirational vision is in place – however it can't just be top-down. You need staff buy-in and commitment. This means involvement in not just decision, but design. It includes co-design, radical knowledge sharing and regular feedback as you work through each phase of your change. It necessitates a different way of thinking. From change team(s) as 'resources' to change team(s) as partners.

USE TARGETED SELF-LABELLING & SELF-ALIGNMENT

We humans lean heavily on psychological shortcuts. One such shortcut is through quick and efficient labelling of ourselves and everyone around us.

'Go-getters', 'addicts', 'bludgers', 'smart', 'funny', 'charismatic', 'extroverted', 'left-brained', 'creative', 'driven'. We sort people into mental boxes. Labels drive not only our perceptions of others but our perceptions of ourselves. We gather small amounts of information and quickly jump to limiting or incorrect conclusions[49].

Maybe you failed a maths test in year 2, do you still think you are poor at maths?

Maybe your high school art teacher admonished your creative spirit, and you suddenly concluded you must be 'a logic based' person.

The truth is we all operate on spectrums, and we are so rarely at the extremes. So, these labels often perform us a dis-service. However, these labels can also be used to encourage and create desired behaviour in our organisations.

You can strategically create a label that makes sense for this group to align with (for example, 'Person X' is our internal expert on 'Topic Y'), and then provide public exposure under that very label. No matter the result of the public exposure, these individuals will start to self-identify under that label.

Use this wisely.

---

[49] Another great spot for an Officespace reference: 'Jump to Conclusions Mat' anyone?

POSITIVE DISRUPTION

The second strategy to building fanaticism is one of surpassing expectations. Consider the last time you recommended something to someone. I'd bet it was because your experience with that thing surpassed your expectations. Or put another way, it fell on the right side of the expectation spectrum (shown below).

Every notch towards Over-Expectation is a minor disruption in someone's mind. It's a subtle re-adjustment. A little pleasant surprise. Kind of like finding a $50 note in the back pocket of a pair of pants you haven't worn in 6 months.

And how do people process and reconcile this mental readjustment?

By talking to others about it.

And that's **exactly** what we want!

Your job with your team(s) is to be bold and do things a little differently. Be cutting edge and subvert the standard systems. Or if non-compliance is the norm, then cross every 't' and dot every 'i'. If the culture is typically hierarchical, then create the feel of a flat structure and run an open floor. Or if the organisation is already typically flat and democratic, then have a strong, clear, decision-focused approach.

No matter your move, make it feel natural! Your change needs to feel different. Different enough that people just **HAVE** to talk about it with their peers to enable their minds to truly process it.

This is positive disruption. And this is what we're after.

Positive disruption coupled with strategic belonging creates strong fanaticism.

Strong fanaticism makes your life easier.

So be bold. Create something different. And reap the rewards.

Maintaining High Momentum

Like an engine under power, your team's momentum can be 'revved higher' through the strategies we just discussed. However, similar to an engine – without proper care, the ongoing friction of everyday work will take its toll on your team's momentum.

Counter this by keeping in mind the two key measures for your team: Hope and Energy.

If you start to see or feel a drop in either of these, then it's likely that one or more of your team(s) are sliding down the Momentum Path. Check in, evaluate where they are, and then reapply the strategies as needed.

The people in your change are responsible for every result your change produces. Don't waste them – build momentum, harness the talent, generate the energy – and watch your results improve out of sight.

VALUABLE CHANGE

Chapter 6: Forge Influential Champions & Communities

Brian Cohen (of Nazareth) - *"Look, you've got it all wrong. You don't need to follow me. You don't need to follow anybody. You've got to think for yourselves. You're all individuals."*

Large Crowd - *"Yes. We're All Individuals!"*

— Monty Python's the Life of Brian

The remainder of the VP model[50] is focused outward from your own team(s). These are:

2. Identify and Enlist Internal Influencers.
3. Engage & Grow through Community.

---

[50] If you don't know what the VP model is, I'd highly recommend backtracking to the first few pages of Chapter 5 and finding out.

IDENTIFY AND ENLIST INTERNAL INFLUENCERS: FIND THE RIGHT PEOPLE IN YOUR ORGANISATION TO RECRUIT TO YOUR CAUSE

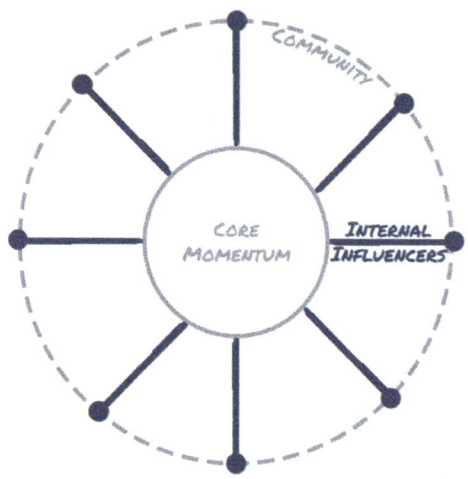

It's time to shift our attention outward. From focusing on our own team(s) to focusing on the people that we are looking to engage and change.

How do we best communicate, enlist and work with these groups of people? Which, depending on the change initiative, can vary from 10 people to 10,000 people.

Well, we could always just airstrike in our communication. Send the same thing to everyone. Have everyone attend every workshop and meeting. Have everyone treated the same. And if you're trying to shift a group of people less than 20 or so, then this is a perfectly valid approach. In essence you are assuming that your target stakeholders are arranged like this:

The scary thing with this one though is that it's often a last-minute airstrike.

> *Hmm... the change is rolling out in a week?*
>
> *Well, I suppose we better tell everyone then...*

But what to do when you're trying to change more than 20 people?

Well, you could cluster them together. Find some common theme and create logical groupings. Then you can create tailored communications and workshops for each of these groups. If blasting everyone equally was an airstrike, then this is analogous to throwing a grenade.

Target grouping (the grenade) is a very common approach in many change initiatives. It assumes your target stakeholders are arranged like this:

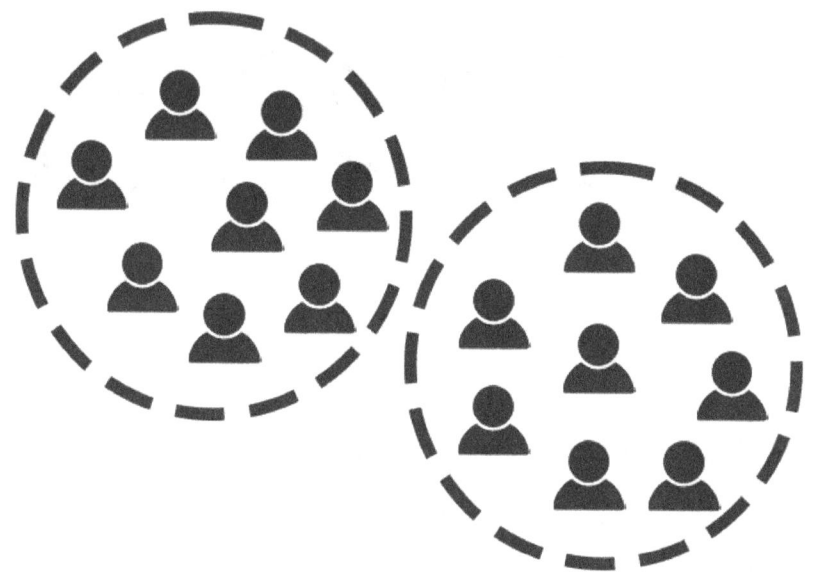

But one day, someone, somewhere realised they could enhance the grenade group method even more. They could use a strategy similar to watchtowers and outposts in the days of medieval war. By enlisting a 'change champion' in each of these groups to hold their banner high and provide guidance to those in their lands, they would both metaphorically save gunpowder and reduce collateral damage. Communications could then be targeted to these change champions, who would then disperse it and represent the change accordingly.

This approach assumes that your target stakeholders are arranged like this:

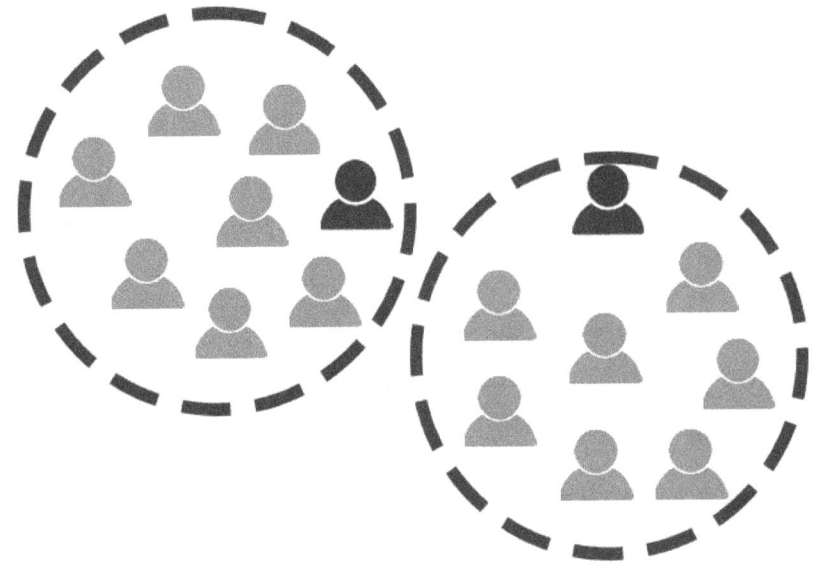

Now don't get me wrong. This is a great approach and is the one used in most medium to large sized change efforts today. But this approach suffers from a fatal flaw:

How do you know that you have the right person enlisted as your change champion?

A Little Detour Through The World of Network Science

To answer this question, let's take a little detour into the world of network science. I promise it'll just be a short trip, and then we'll come right back to exploring amazing ways to accelerate your change uptake.

Take a moment with me and think about how you use the internet. If I asked you to go to my website *(www.valuablechange.com)*, how would you get there?

Would you manually type in the URL? Or would you type my business name, **Valuable Change Co.,** into Google, Bing, LinkedIn or similar? And route in that way?

Now what about if instead of getting to my business webpage, I asked you to find information about the feeding habits of a flamingo?

Would you go direct to *https://en.wikipedia.org/wiki/Flamingo#Behavior_and_ecology*, or would you use one of the search and social engines above?

Your answers to these questions are useful. They give a little insight into how we access and share information.

Generally, if we know exactly where we want to go then we do so. When we don't, or when the URL is too long to bother typing[51] we

---

[51] The reward of direct access vs the pain of typing the longer URL no longer makes sense. See, the Value Equation is everywhere!

lean heavily on a *'connection hub'* to find what we need... And with the internet growing at exponential rates, we'd be silly not to.

What's interesting for us here though, is that a leading Professor of Network Science Albert-László Barabási also looked at the structure of the internet. In his book *'Linked'*, he outlines the nature of most complex and advanced networks.

To summarise and simplify what is a fascinating read; the internet looks something like this:

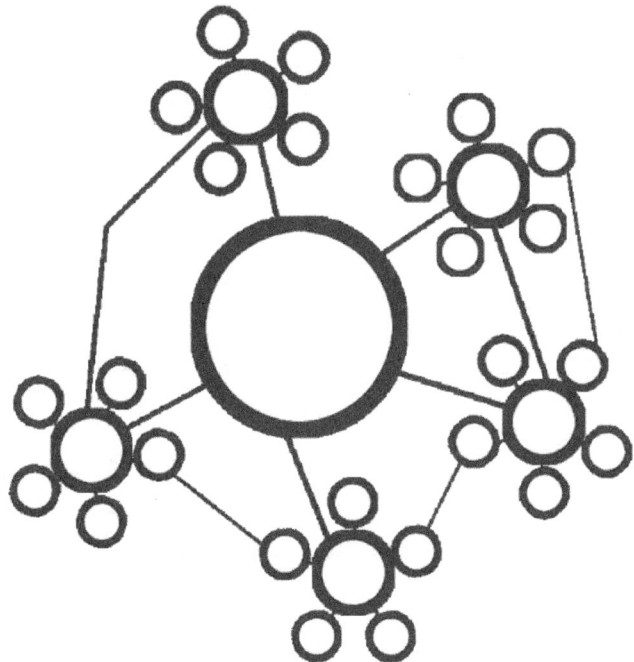

That is, complex networks form and follow hub and node patterns. In the diagram on the previous page, the size of the circle represents the number of connections each node has.

In fact, Albert-László Barabási found that networks follow a power law distribution curve. Without delving too deep into the world of mathematics here, (after all, I did promise this would just be a short excursion from our change discussions) – A power law distribution tells us that the vast majority of network nodes have very few links and a tiny number of the nodes have a huge number of links.

Which, when you think about the internet, is no real surprise.

Consider Google – It's just one web node, with links to hundreds of billions of webpages.

Bing – Similar story.

Amazon – One web node, with over 353 million products (only 12 million of which are through Amazon directly). That's potentially links to over 341 million other websites, assuming a one-to-one product to seller link ratio.

Facebook – Even by ignoring the personal pages, Facebook has over 60 million active business pages. If we assume just half of them have external websites, that's another 1 to 30 million node to link ratio there.

Seems this power ratio holds true.

But we're talking about information storage here. What does this have to do with people?

Well... everything.

I'm sure you've heard of the concept of six degrees of separation.

In case you haven't:

> "Six degrees of separation is the idea that all people on average are six, or fewer, social connections away from each other. As a result, a chain of "friend of a friend" statements can be made to connect any two people in a maximum of six steps."[52]

And maybe, if you're a cinephile, you've heard of Six Degrees of Kevin Bacon?

Where:

> "The object of the game is to start with any actor or actress who has been in a movie and connect them to Kevin Bacon in the smallest number of links possible. Two people are linked if they've been in a movie together."[53]

What's interesting is that both of these theories have been tested and proven.

Six degrees of separation has been tested multiple times, with one of the latest being held in the early 2000s. Researchers at Columbia University pulled together over 60,000 people from 166 different countries and assigned them one of eighteen target people. Participants were asked to try to contact that person by emailing someone they already knew that would potentially be 'closer' to their assigned target. The targets were varied, from an

---

[52] A quote from yet another internet hub: Wikipedia. *https://en.wikipedia.org/wiki/Six_degrees_of_separation*
[53] *https://oracleofbacon.org/help.php*

Aussie policeman, to an American professor to a Norwegian veterinarian.

The results: Most cases took between 5 and 7 emails to contact the target.

...Which really is just a funny way of saying 6.

And what about the Kevin Bacon game?

Well, it's a fairly easy problem for a computer to solve. Especially when you feed it all the data from the Internet Movie Database (IMDB). And in the mid-90s a bunch of programmers did so.

The result: Kevin Bacon is, on average, less than 3 links away from any other movie actor or actress.

But how is this possible?

There are hundreds of thousands, if not millions, of movie actors and actresses. And there are over 7.6 billion people in the world – and yet, we can connect any two of them with just 3 and 6 links respectively?

"THEY ARE CONNECTORS"

In his bestselling book, The Tipping Point, Malcolm Gladwell describes a simple experiment that he ran. He first made a list of 248 surnames from a Manhattan phone book. He then approached various groups and asked them to count how many people they knew that shared a surname with one of the 248 that were listed. Multiples counted too – so if you knew three people with the last name 'Smith', then that was 3 points. He approached over 400 people this way and the results shocked him.

The averages were within expectations, but in each group of people there were some with scores that were improbably high. His conclusion was that

> *"Sprinkled among every walk of life... are a handful of people with a truly extraordinary knack of making friends and acquaintances. They are Connectors."*

So how can we traverse the world's 7.6 billion people in just 6 steps?

Through connectors.

But here's the thing that Malcolm glosses over in his findings: these people were found in EACH of his groups. That's because, as Barabási points out in his own work, these connective hubs are a feature of complex networks.

And our society is a complex network.

As are our organisations.

Being a feature of our societal network means that this hub and node pattern is loosely fractal. It is infinitely self-similar across different scales.

In other words, these social connectors exist in groups of a hundred people the same way they do in groups of one million.

So, no matter the size of your organisation – there are people that are bringing that network together. These people are your connectors, or more importantly for you, your Internal Influencers.

Internal Influencers: The Connective Tissue Of Your Organisation

'Social Influencer' – a career that didn't exist just a few years ago is now a rapidly growing arm of the marketing efforts of businesses worldwide. With increases in dedicated influencer spend each year, projections suggest that between 5 and 10 billion dollars were spent on influencers in 2020 alone.

It's clear that this group hold real power.

Social Influencers can take a multitude of forms – from beauty and fitness Instagram celebrities to video game streamers on Twitch or Vloggers on YouTube.[54]

But not everyone wants to be an Instagram star. There are many who want to excel in finance, marketing, project management, leadership, or some other form of valuable service.

It's these people that form the connective tissue of our organisations. It's these people that play the network-necessary role of connector. And ultimately, it's these people that we need on our side for maximum change adoption.

---

[54] And even listing these channels here will slowly date this book as the brands grow, mature and then eventually fade away.

Bringing us back to our grenade and watchtower analogies from earlier. We no longer need to assume what our target stakeholder groups look like. We now know they look like this:

The big question here is how do we find these people?

Finding Your Internal Influencers With Just Two Questions

To find your Internal Influencers, we just need to take one more detour. I promise this one will be shorter than the last.

This time we are heading to the world of sociology. Not for answers, but rather for inspiration.

Now that we know the pattern that underpins human networks (hubs and nodes), I want to pose you a hypothetical challenge.

Pretend you are a researcher studying the homeless at your nearest city. There is usually no simple way to identify the number of homeless people living there, let alone any usable way to get their respective contact details.

What would you do?

Well perhaps you have a little sociology or statistics training, so you decide to adopt a strategy that researchers often use in these types of situations: a technique called snowball sampling.

Snowball sampling is quite simple. Researchers recruit initial study participants and then ask those initial participants to recruit additional people to be in the study. Using this approach, the sample size "snowballs" larger and larger as each additional participant recruits more participants.

Theoretical snowball sampling looks like this:

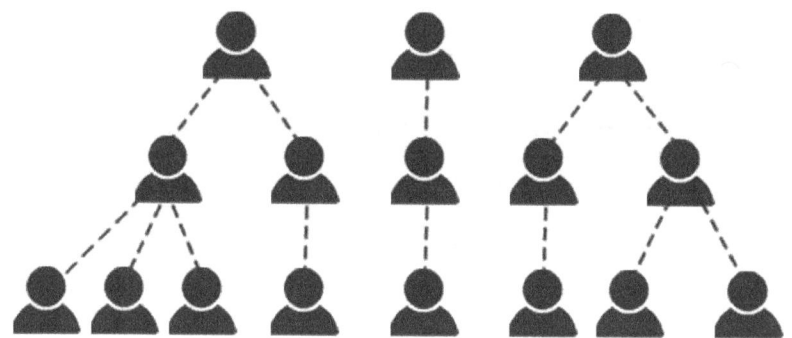

...A little like a Multi-Level-Marketing scheme.

It's a great technique and works well for hard to quantify populations like sex workers and the homeless.

But our organisations are usually not so hard to quantify. Most of your target stakeholders will be listed on a directory somewhere and will usually have both a real world and electronic mail address.

It's not the sampling technique we care about here – but rather the idea of a snowball gathering in size.

Think about the reality of running one of these types of studies. In all likelihood, the same names are going to keep coming up again and again.

This means that in reality, it probably looks closer to this:

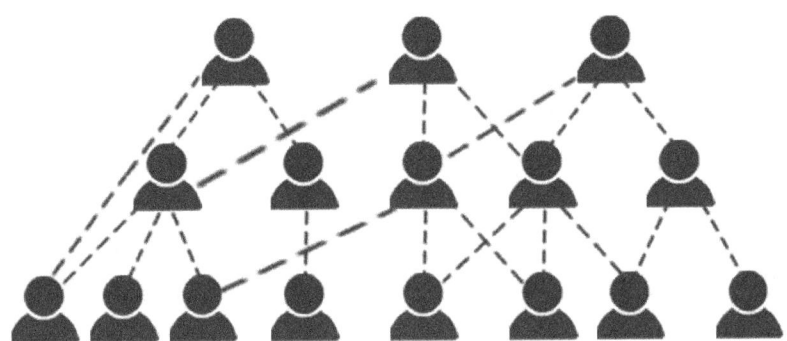

Those overlaps? That happens when people are nominated multiple times. Someone that is overlapping is one of those connectors we talked about earlier. And in your organisations, those overlaps are your Internal Influencers.

So how do we find your Internal Influencers? Well, we ask their peers to identify them for you.

Let's make a little assumption. Let's assume that your internal influencers are found at the intersection of two key types of people:

- **Type 1: The Value Adders.** Value Adders are people that others love to work with because they carry more than their load, add something useful to every engagement and love to do so. They are the Amazon's or Shopify's of your organisation.

- **Type 2: The Information Brokers.** Information Brokers are the local go-to points for all relevant news, updates and (non-detrimental, honest) gossip. They are the Google's of your organisation.

This means that for any group that you are looking to identify the key internal influencers in, you merely need to run a simple survey that asks just 2 questions:

1) If you could work with any three people from across the <group/branch/organisation>, on any project, who would they be?

2) If you needed to be filled in on organisational news, key updates, or gossip, who would you go to first?

Then all you need to do is collate the data. A simple tally of the names is enough to get started. The more times a name comes up, the higher that person's internal influence.

Simple right?

FOR THE DATA NERDS

For those data nerds amongst us (you know who you are), feel free to further query the information. Some other lenses to consider when examining the data include (but aren't limited to):

- Which organisational areas have the most influencers?
- Who are the highest influencers across multiple groups, within certain sets of interesting parameters?
- Which influencers have the most inter-team connections?
- Are the influencers slanted towards formal leadership roles or are they typically peer level?

ENGAGE & GROW THROUGH COMMUNITY: THE ESSENCE OF A GREAT COMMUNITY

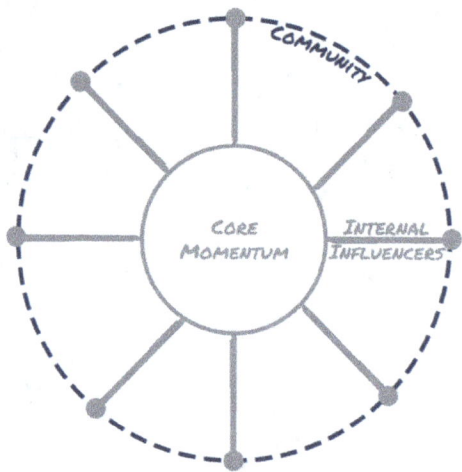

The final step of the VP model is to build a community around your change direction with your now secured influencers at the helm. The community forms a crucial role in our change efforts as it proactively provides peer-level support structures for your target stakeholders. This is something they are going to seek out anyway. So, for those of us leading Valuable Change, it's worthwhile knowing how to create an environment that is slanted towards our change goals, rather than leaving it to the whims of chaotic chance.

The problem is... most organisational communities' suck.

THE ESSENCE OF A GREAT COMMUNITY

It might surprise you, but I can differentiate between communities that succeed and those that don't in just one sentence. (And if you read Chapter 4: Stack the Value Equation[55] then you should be able to as well.)

The key difference between communities that succeed and those that don't is the net balance of the Value Equation.

A typical organisational community falls flat because it doesn't stack the Value Equation in its favour. In other words, the events and benefits of the community don't outweigh the pain and effort required to turn up, delay work, and persevere through awkward conversations.

So how do we stack the equation?

---

[55] If you did skip it, then I highly recommend you go back and read it. This section will make far more sense if you do.

A Rewarding Community

There are 3 key avenues to boost the 'reward' column of your community's Value Equation:

Exclusivity

Your community can't be open to everyone. Counter-intuitively there needs to be barriers to entry. While these may not necessarily be financial (although they can be), a minimum criteria underpinning community acceptance is crucial. While this does increase the pain of access, it also ensures that the community consists of the right people.

For a change Community that means targeting thought-leader style professionals who are actively interested in organisational success.

With exclusivity we safeguard against dilution of value. We raise the lowest common denominator, which in turn, raises the value of the content you can and should explore. Exclusivity also sets your community up nicely to maximise the next two reward avenues.

Reputation

Your community must be held in high regard. It must be synonymous with success. The idea here is that anyone involved in your community receives a reputation boost simply by being connected to it. One of the best ways to achieve this is to identify high performers within your organisation and enlist them.

You should also put effort into leveraging popular and impressive names from the industry and have them speak to your members. You will increase your members' reputation just by correlating your community's name with a market leader. You want your members to be able to casually drop humblebrags[56] like:

> "My mind is spinning. I still can't believe I got to meet the head of NASA's rocket program at the ‹your change name here› Community Event yesterday!"

In short - you must provide ways for your community members to have a genuine advantage over those who aren't members.

EDGY CONTENT

There is nothing worse than boring content. Want people to stop contributing to the community? Feed them yet another session on how to track capital expenses or how to use the new time tracking tool.

Content must be interesting. Instead of a session on the value of your new processes– what about a session on *'How to avoid and shortcut our new processes'?*

Can't come up with anything interesting? Ask an author to come talk. Or approach an industry legend. In other words – don't be afraid to outsource it. Worst case, I'm sure there's a consulting

---

[56] Merriam-Webster: humblebrag: *to make a seemingly modest, self-critical, or casual statement or reference that is meant to draw attention to one's admirable or impressive qualities or achievements.*

firm out there that would happily pull together the newest industry trends for you every quarter and present on it.

The point here is simple. **Don't be boring.** Don't just say the same old tired things. If you have pursued both the Exclusivity and Reputation avenues, then you will have a membership of high performers.

Help them be even better.

A Few Other Notes On Community

Now, before we close this talk of community, here are a few other notes you should seriously consider.

- Your community should have a brand. Something memorable and easy to verbally share. Your imagination really is the limit here, but as always, remember that simplicity is key.

- Maximise availability for members. Make the community hard to get into, but open and easy once you are in. Feel free to leverage the many social tools within your organisation here. MS Teams, Facebook for Workplace are common examples.

- Opt for more impressive events, less often, rather than less impressive events, more often.

- There is massive value in connectivity. Not just to industry superstars, but also between organisational superstars.

Create opportunities for their connection (without holding yet another networking event... *YAWN*).

- Ensure the small details are congruent with the image you're building. If your community is exclusive and has a high reputation - don't just put together the cheapest venues and food options. No one wants yet another Costco platter. However, a breakfast event at the local Hyatt – now that's another story.

- Give the community the time and investment it deserves. **DON'T** take on a community unless you have the ability to adequately support and promote it. This means at least a part time role allocation within your change team and an appropriately sized budget to put behind it.

- And finally, you **will** have to spend money on this to succeed.

But Wait There's More! Bonus Tactic: How To Truly Shift Capability

Before we wrap this section up, I want to share one more tactic. A little bonus add-on if you will.

Many change efforts have an objective along the lines of 'increasing capability' or similar. What this normally means is some sort of training program. And there's no doubt about it, training is big business.

Let's delve a little deeper into an example that I'm rather well acquainted with - project management training.

AXELOS - the key UK based provider of project management best practice - has certified over 5 million people since its establishment in 2013. The Project Management Institute (PMI) has certified over 1.4 million people, regularly generating a yearly revenue of over $220M. Then there are the hundreds of thousands of certified agile practitioners, from SCRUM to SAFE[57] to the 50+ other variations.

Without a doubt, that's a lot of certificates.

But does all this training make a difference? Well, yes, and no.

It's important to be clear here. It is not the new training offerings that are the concern. There are many extremely good ideas, concepts and courses out there.

---

[57] Yes, it seems that project management organisations really do like their acronyms...

It is who organisations are sending on training, and the support network they return to.

Consider this: when an experienced project veteran attends a new training course, they learn new techniques and approaches, and ultimately end up with more 'tools in their toolbox'. This is great.

It is the training for the inexperienced 'project-newbie' staff that falls notably short. What we end up with is a staff member with plenty of theoretical knowledge but without the experience to adequately translate it into the imperfect reality of projects. This results in either:

1) the staff member making a valiant effort to incorporate a few elements into their approach, assuming something is better than nothing,

    or, what we see more often,

2) a complete abandon of the new theory as 'excessively burdensome', 'not useful', or 'getting in the way of real work'.

Bringing this back to your broader change efforts – I see this same mistake being made in training program after training program. This idea that a single eLearning module or a couple hours of classroom training is enough to drive zero-to-hero levels of capability is somewhat frightening.

We humans just don't work like that…

So, What Works?
How Do We Sustainably Increase Capability?

Before we can address this question, we need to understand the nature of how we humans grow and progress. To do this, let's take another little excursion.

This time to the Australian stock market.

In its whole, the Australian Stock Exchange (ASX) represents both the cumulative investment decisions of over 7 million people and the totality of growth of the largest Australian businesses. For this reason alone, the ASX is a unique representation of human growth - but there's a further bonus - the market is regularly priced. This means we can graphically plot collective human growth and progress.

The index that tracks the largest 200 ASX listed stocks (the XJO) closed out 1992 at a value of $1,564. The following 29 years saw incredible progress and in June 2021 the XJO closed out at just over $7,300. If we were to plot that simply on a two-axis price/time graph it would look something like the figure on the next page.

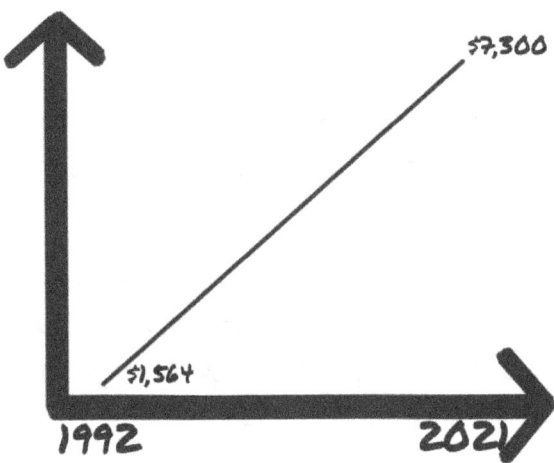

But that straight line is misleading. Reality was messier, it was imperfect. Something closer to reality would look something like this:

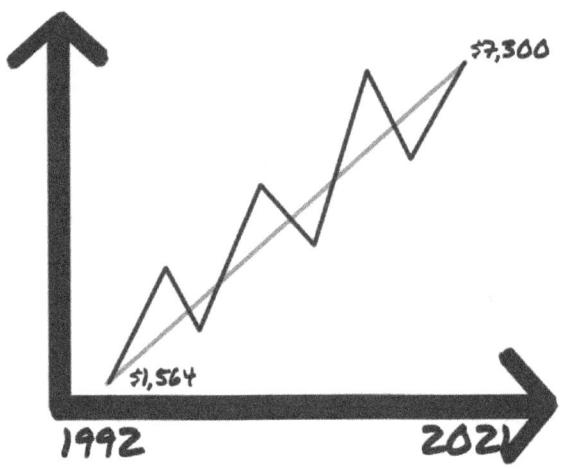

What we see are waves.

We humans grow in waves.

This is where training fundamentally falls short. It is a 'once and done' solution, that simply doesn't achieve the capability growth it seeks to.

Analysing the growth wave pattern, we can channel our inner Sherlock Holmes and deduce what might work. The waves seem to start with a 'growth phase' followed by a 'grounding and reinforcement phase'. To help visualise this I've added some labels below.

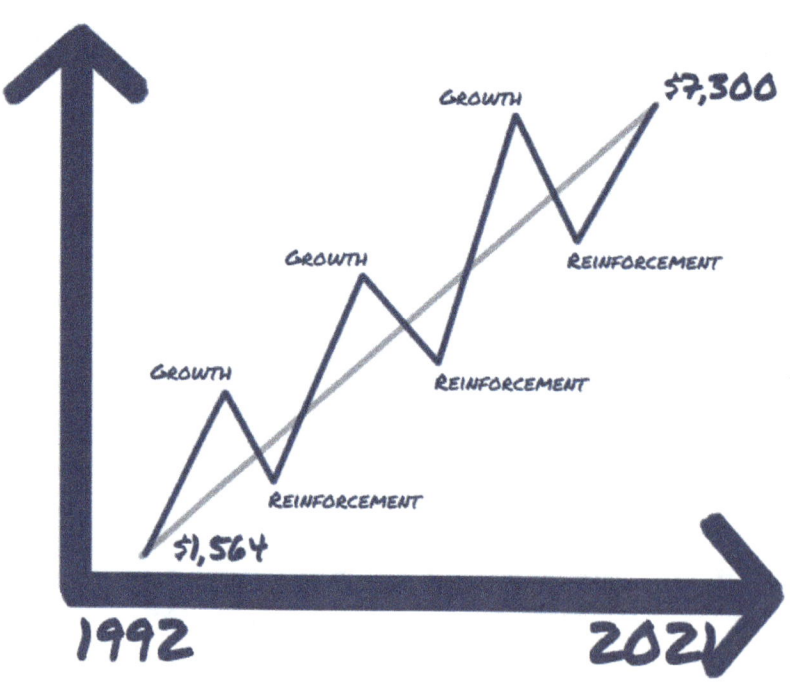

Now, if you have ever had the joy of witnessing a small child learn and grow, the nature of these growth waves will be familiar. The wave cycle is particularly easy to see in little ones of toddler age (2-3yrs). Anyone who has ever experienced sleep, reading or toilet training with a little one can attest to this very cycle. A few days forward, a couple of days back, then a few days forward to a higher level, then a couple more back.

Grow, then regress to cement and reinforce, then grow again.

THE 4R'S OF RAPID CAPABILITY

This same growth pattern doesn't just apply to toddlers but rather to humans of all ages. This pattern is how you build true capability improvements through your organisation.

I'll break it down for you into 4 steps. I tend to call them **the 4R's.**

First, you need to create a target capability **Roadmap** to act as a compass for progression.

Second, you need to create growth. This is the **Reach** phase. Think 'kickstart' here. This is a short term, focused effort to establish disciplines that did not exist or weren't previously sustained. This is not the time to try to implement everything. Keep it simple, keep it focused, and most importantly keep it clear. You are aiming to create motion and confidence.

Third, you move into the **Regress** phase. This is where you use testing and exposure to trigger small regressions. By challenging the progress made in the previous growth push you can identify faulty foundations, remove any overconfidence, and clarify the true new skills and capabilities built.

Fourth, you then immediately move into a **Reinforce** phase. The aim in this phase is to pour cement on what is going well, and fill any holes created through the regression phase. Peer to peer support or coaching is extremely effective here. So too are communities of practice and self-service learning.

You then cycle back to the next Reach phase, kickstarting to an entirely new level of capability – in line with your progression Roadmap.

This ebb and flow cycle leaves 'once and done' style training in the dust. So next time you need to drive new capability, look beyond 'once and done' style training.

After all, no one is really all that impressed with one hit wonders.

RALLYING IS HARD WORK

As you may be starting to see over the last 2 chapters, rallying is hard work.

My advice here is don't shortchange yourself. Don't find yourself with only subject matter experts - leaving no one to create a solid change brand or message to rally behind.

As such, when you are designing the team that will support your change journey, I highly recommend including a communications or marketing specialist.

Similarly, when seeking or allocating budget for this endeavour, ensure you put aside money for events and marketing.

You will thank me later.

Chapter 7:
Value Balance Your Change Support

"There's a fine line between support and stalking and let's all stay on the right side of that."

- Joss Whedon

We've talked about building a strong change core, installing driver's aids, and ensuring our drivers (people) are in top shape. It's now time to talk about our pit crews.

Whether you call it a Project Management Office (PMO), a Governance Team, an Agile Hub, a Delivery Excellence Group or one of the many other derivatives – the truth is that the vast majority of changes need some form of support.

This is because our changes don't operate in a vacuum. They operate in an organisation. An organisation that usually has other things happening at the same time. **Your change support function is the conduit between your change efforts and your organisation's bureaucratic friction.** Whether it's reporting, governance, audits, forecasting, risk profiling, investment analysis or one of the other 50+ things a change support function can do.

I've written an entire other book[58] about how to ensure maximum value from these change support functions, so I'll avoid going into great detail here. If you're interested in the practical application of what we cover here, then I suggest you pick up that book. But as tempting as it would be for me to say *"Go read that book"* – it just wouldn't be doing you justice because an effective support function is a crucial part of the success of medium and large change efforts.

But there is a major problem most organisations face here.

Most change support functions fail.

They become burdensome overheads. Unwieldy value-vacuums - sucking in time and effort from those around them and producing nothing worthwhile from it.

Thankfully not all change support functions operate this way. The truly successful ones operate with a different mindset.

One of **service**.

---

[58] Creating High Value PMOs – see www.valuablechange.com for more information.

The Secret Behind Effective Change Support

Let's just jump straight into it. Here's the secret.

An effective Change Support Function is centred on service, not compliance.

For many of you this may seem all too obvious, but for many it will feel blasphemous.

No matter your reaction, what I've found is that the most effective change support functions operate at the intersection of high trust and high value.

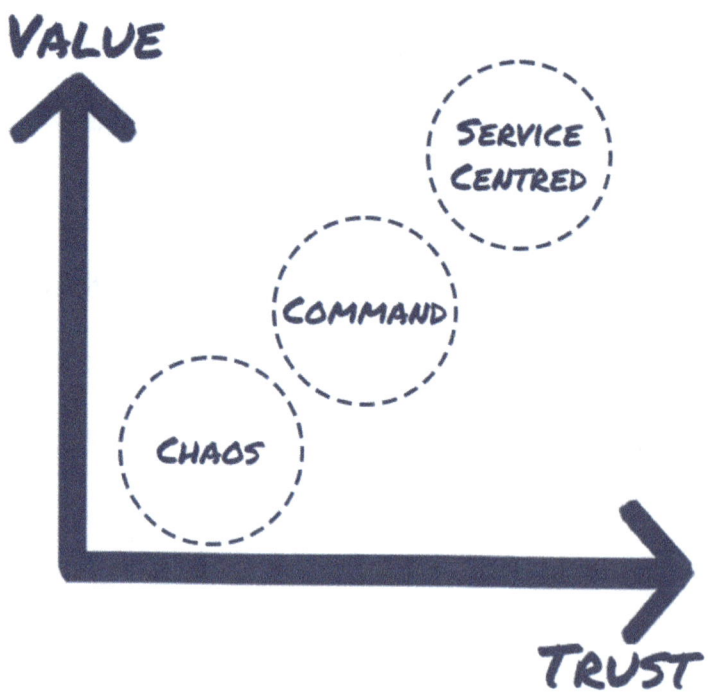

Why Command & Control Isn't The Answer

I do a lot of work with change support functions and what I'm seeing is that most of them are stuck in what I call the Administrative Death Cycle. (Grim name, I know...)

But here's the fascinating thing. This cycle applies to almost any support, governance, or compliance function in your organisations. So, if you're running a change support function, or some other form of business oversight, it's worth being intimately aware of this cycle... and how to break out of it.

There are 6 key phases in the Admin Death Cycle. Let's step through the journey together.

First, There is No Clear, Informed Picture of Project Progress

This is our first state. Projects exist but are generally free to operate independently and in their own way.

Common characteristics that are often found in this state, include:

- A lack of project investment logic,
- A lack of project confidence,
- A lack of consistent process, and
- Low project management maturity.

Usually there is a mix of these. An organisation may exist like this for a while, but over time the frustrations that stem from chaos build up until someone with enough clout (and a budget) says:

"No one knows what is going on! We need Support!"

Which leads us to our next state.

A Change Support Function is Stood Up

Its initial focus can vary but it normally starts with an effort to build consistent processes and some sort of reporting. Typically, it has a mission along the lines of:

"We will drive consistency and visibility".

So, the Support Function takes the next logical step.

It Produces Metrics and Reports

To achieve its mission, the Change Support Function starts producing reports and metrics to monitor the work and projects under its remit. What it finds is often a mixed bag. Some projects are healthy. Others aren't.

The issue is that after a few months of consistent processes and pretty reports, the unhealthy projects don't seem to be improving.

So, the Support Function thinks:

"The projects aren't improving... We need more assurance."

RIGOUR INCREASES -
MORE METRICS, MORE TESTS, GREATER HURDLES

The Support Function, eager to please its stressed executives, dials up its health checks and assurance programs.

More checks, more gates, more oversight.

Which of course creates

...More delays,

...Slower processes,

...And ultimately overburdens both the support team(s) and the projects.

Suddenly, this function, which was meant to be supporting change delivery, has found itself 'policing' projects. It has created a 'command and control' culture. Smothered with bureaucracy, the projects naturally think:

> *"This is overly cumbersome."*

Which eventually leads to discontent.

Project Managers Subvert the 'Support' Systems and Complain in Corridors to Project Executives

Gradually it begins. The shadow processes. The work arounds.

Projects subvert the now cumbersome processes. Despite the persistent, but now, often cynical attempts at driving adherence – projects are now resorting to seeking forgiveness rather than permission just so things still get done!

Slowly but surely the Support Function is neutered. Then one day someone with a notable amount of office clout mentions that:

> *"We would be faster without the Support. We are doing it ourselves. Their team is a hindrance – and an expensive one at that!"*

And just like that, the fate of the Function is sealed. It is death-bound.

Function Disbanded

The Support Function is closed down. Contractors are let go and employees are redeployed. It is buried in the organisational graveyard.

The grave is unmarked.

No stone is risen.

No songs are sung.

...A couple of years then pass, and a new executive comes in. They look around and notice the lack of a clear, informed picture of projects. They think:

> *"No one knows what is going on! We need Support!"*

And off we go again!

VISUALISING THE CYCLE

The figure on the next page demonstrates the clear progression through each of these states.

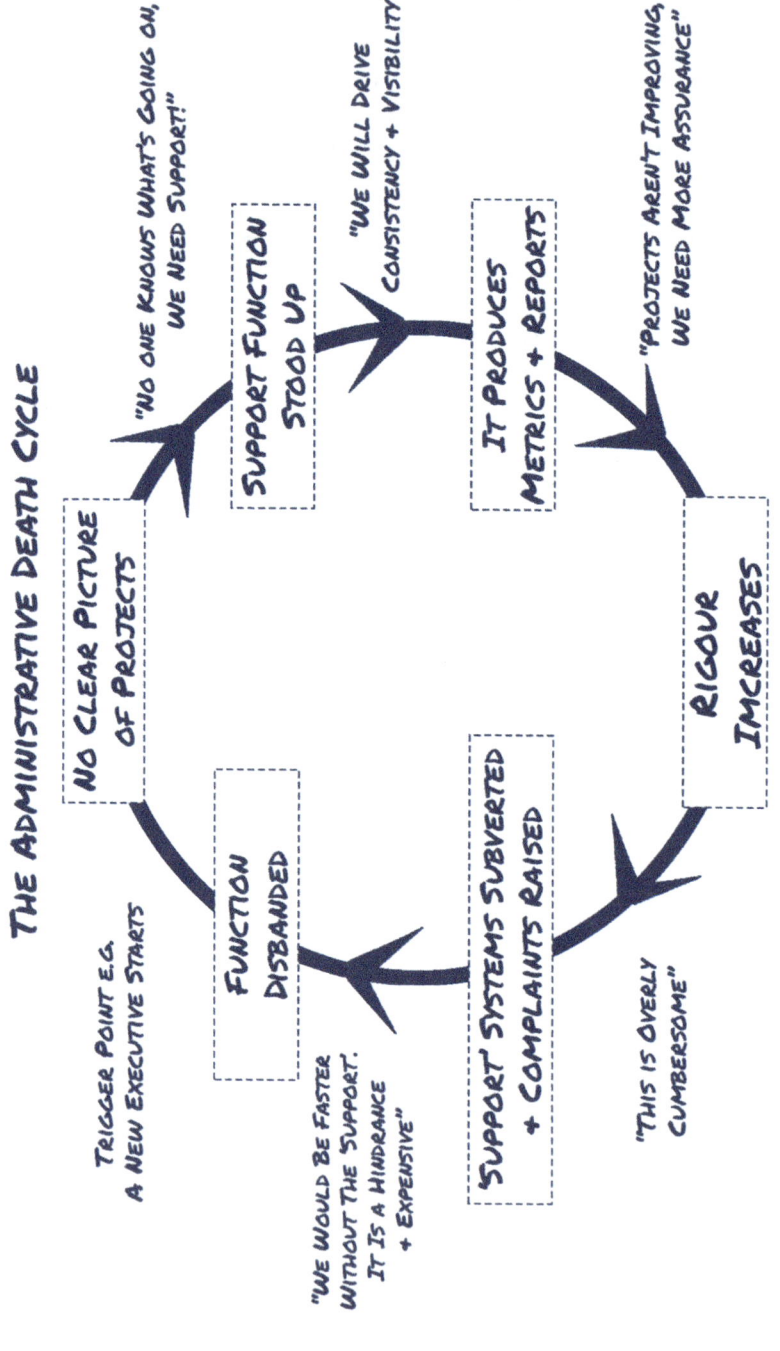

An Imbalanced Equation

The cycle is clear. And using our Value Equation from Chapter 4 – the reasoning for the slow descent into ineffectiveness should also be clear.

There's a Net Negative Value Equation. To give you a sense of what this looks like for most of these Change Support Functions – let's look at one of the most common tasks that falls into their remit: Project Reporting.

The Value Equation for Project Reporting within most Support Functions looks something like this:

PROCESS	REWARD	PAIN ENDURED
Project Reporting	- Avoid being hassled for reports. - The project turns up on a dashboard.	- Potentially several hours of data collation and wordsmithing.

Net Result: Painful.

Breaking The Cycle

So how does a Change Support Function break out of this cycle?

Simple.

We need to break the fatal assumption that greater assurance equals greater projects.

It just doesn't.

The key thing we must adjust is our thinking. We must avoid falling into the trap of

> *"The projects aren't improving... We need more assurance."*

And instead, we need to pivot to

> *"The projects aren't improving... What new value can we offer to increase their capability?"*

It is only through this new way of thinking that we can enter a new cycle. One that helps rather than hinders.

We will enter 'The High Value Service Cycle'.

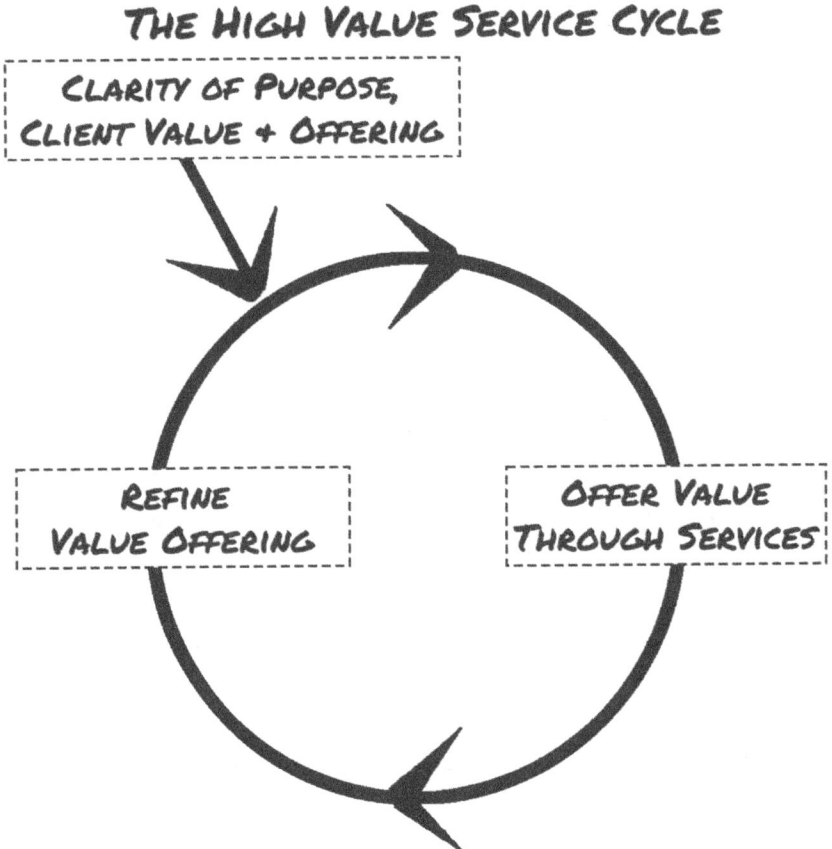

The Path To The High Value Service Cycle

A High Value Change Support Function needs absolute clarity over 3 key areas:

Key Area 1: A Clear Purpose

Why does your Support Function exist?

What is its purpose?

Its purpose must be so clear that everyone can answer it instinctively. An absurdly clear purpose helps set expectations on what the Support Function will be excellent at, while ringfencing its scope to avoid the cacophony of distractions on its way.

The Power of Purpose

Let's take a little detour to touch on what a good, clear purpose can help you achieve.

In 2008 a group of friends hanging out in their living room came across two numbers that truly shocked them.

- 900 million people across the world didn't have access to clean drinking water.
- Globally, countries with plenty of safe drinking water spent over $50 Billion a year on bottled water.

Initially this group of friends found this polarity ridiculous – until they had a bold idea.

'What if we could connect these two numbers?!'

'What if we could start a business selling bottled water where 100% of the profits went to connecting these 900 Million people with clean drinking water?'.

And so, 'Thankyou.' was born. Despite only having $1000 to their names, this group of friends quickly secured a bottler, packager and distributor. Within 5 years, through sheer public driven momentum, they had grown to 14 products and were stocked in most of Australia's largest retailers and supermarkets.

Within 10 years they had launched a bestselling book based on their own start up story and had used the book to make an international expansion.

'Thankyou.' are clear on their purpose.

> *"End poverty in this lifetime".*

Without clarity of purpose, these friends would still be sitting in that living room – appalled at the numbers on the TV in front of them.

FINDING YOUR SUPPORT FUNCTION'S PURPOSE

How do we get to the heart of your Change Support Function's purpose?

By answering 2 simple questions:

1. Why does it exist?
   (What was the catalyst for its creation?), and
2. What makes it special?
   (What makes it different from any other part of the organisation?)

KEY AREA 2: CLARITY OF THEIR STAKEHOLDER'S PROBLEM(S)

A Change Support Function has a clear understanding of the problem(s) they are solving for their stakeholders. When I say stakeholders here, I'm not talking about the stakeholders of your Change – but rather the groups of people that your Change Support Function are supporting. This often includes groups inside and outside of your change team(s).

To achieve clarity here, there are 4 key questions to answer for each supported group:

- Who are we serving?
- What problem are we solving (for them)?
- What does success look like (for them)?
- How does this help them?

Key Area 3: Clarity of its Service Offering

Your Change Support Function must have a clear service offering that solves its stakeholders key needs, while meeting its own purpose.

Your Change Support Function must ask, and answer:

- How do we create success for those we are supporting?
- How will we create the environment needed?
- When and how will we provide guidance, training and hands on support?
- What's our internal aptitude for these support services?
- What skills and systems are required to offer the services?
- How will our Function's stakeholders access the services?
- Are the services a net positive, or net negative Value Equation?

Key Area 4: Ongoing, Service-Focused Improvement

The final step for our Change Support Functions is to embed the following 3 key questions into their daily, weekly and monthly thinking:

1. How do we increase the quality of our change support services?
2. How do we decrease the pain our stakeholders feel in accessing the services? and
3. How do we reduce our own effort to offer these services?

A Final Note on Change Support

Some projects need support functions of 15 people. Others need the support of just one or two. Others don't need any at all, and just ask their delivery staff to do it.

So, here's a few words of advice:

Don't under-estimate the workload that bureaucratic friction can create. Anticipate it before-hand.

Similarly, don't underestimate the value of a helping hand and a clear set of tools and frameworks to operate under.

Finally, if you are going to have a Change Support Function – ensure it lives and breathes by these two mottos:

1. Service over compliance.
2. Maximise reward while reducing pain.

The Change Support Function that embeds these two ideals deep into its core will provide that much needed lubrication for your change's gears. It'll be the pit crew that gets you back in the race.

Ultimately, it'll accelerate and strengthen your change efforts, buffering the bureaucratic friction of the rest of the organisation.

And that's no small feat.

PART THREE:
YOUR NEXT MOVE

VALUABLE CHANGE

Chapter 8: Shift To Valuable Change

"Be water, my friend."

- Bruce Lee

The great thing about the information, techniques and strategies in this book is that you can deploy any of them at any time in your change to enhance your results. While there is a loosely linear relationship between them, there are no hard dependencies from one to another.

That said, you are best placed to strengthen and accelerate your change using the 2-step process we outlined in Chapter 2. That is, Build the Core, then Drive the Core.

Build the Core → Drive the Core →

There's a very simple reason for this, and it's aligned with the scenario we covered in Chapter 5 – that is, the attitude of your server affects your experience at a restaurant. In essence, your server's attitude ripples into yours. If we delve deeper into that hypothetical, we may find that perhaps the start of that ripple was a restaurant manager who was having a bad day and took it out on your server just a few minutes before you walked in. And so, it ripples outwards to your server, then to you, and potentially through you to your friends or family.

The same is at play with our change initiatives.

Unfortunately, I can't name names here, but let me tell you the story of the change that never happened.

A large Australian Government Department[59] had agreed to take on an admittedly ambitious venture. It was going to centralise the backbone IT systems across the public sector and then provide them back as a 'shared service'. This would save the Australian Government billions of dollars in duplicated licensing, overlapping support costs and process inefficiencies.

This project was no small fry. A true behemoth project.

Unfortunately, this project had a major problem. Its core was weak. Very weak. It had fallen prey to the inverse clarity and cost relationship we covered back in Chapter 1. Which is the same as building on a fluid foundation. An unstable core meant instability throughout.

To give you a sense of the instability we are talking about here. Over the first 3 months of this multi-year change, it had 5 different executive owners. At one stage it was 3 in 3 weeks. The entire

---

[59] Yes, another one. Seems these large Government Departments have some of the best change-disaster stories!

leadership structure was a revolving door. Which would have been endurable if the change core was clear and solid.

But it wasn't.

Like the restaurant manager having a bad day, this instability rippled.

First the team started questioning those core elements:

- Why are we doing this?
- How are we going to prove those outlandish savings claims?
- What are we even doing?

The failure to answer these questions rippled forward, to all those involved in the change itself.

Momentum and morale levels – which had started with hopeful excitement, dropped to fearful and then despair. Rituals fell away and reporting structures fell apart as confusion took hold. Those in their change support function, their PMO, resorted to just doing the work for those around them. Reporting as they were instructed to: that *'The project was tracking Green',* despite the mass instability and shaky foundations.

Finally, the instability rippled further forward again. This time outside the change. Key stakeholders across the broader government started to see the shaky façade. Agreements fell apart. Pilot agencies pulled out. The media were like attack dogs – pouncing on their flailing prey – and controversial articles spread through key news sites.

Finally, after 2 years, an unspeakable amount of money, 6 different 'high end' consulting firms[60] and 4 complete leadership reshuffles, the change initiative was stripped away from this Government Department and handed to another.

The ripple was complete.

The project was a failure.

Now, as gut-wrenchingly familiar this story is, it's also quite instructive. Both useless change and Valuable Change starts from within then ripples outward.

This is how you shift to Valuable Change – you start within and ripple out.

---

[60] Yes, all the usual suspects.

Collating the various strategies within this book, your ripple looks like this:

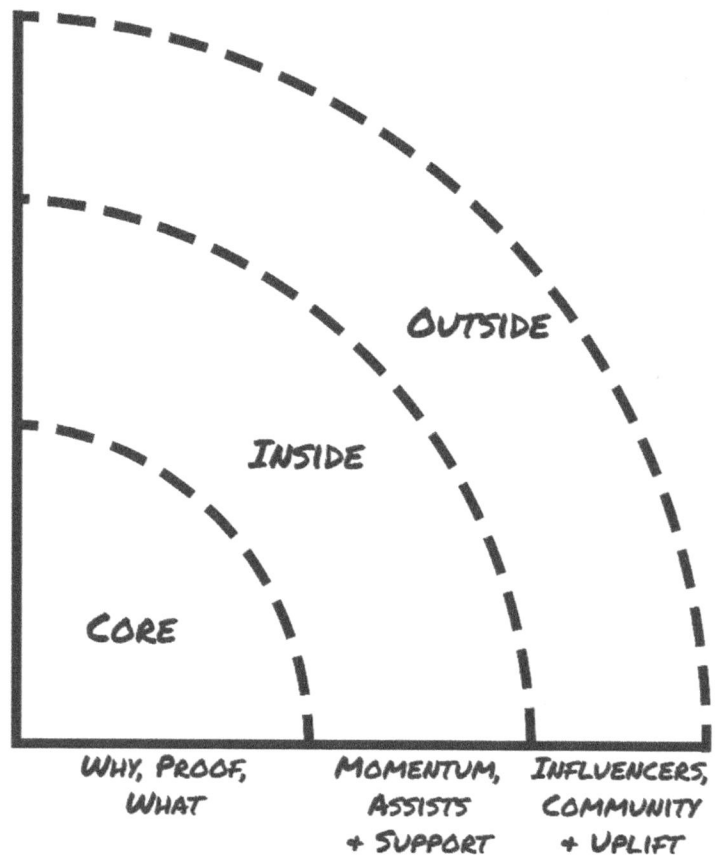

It's crucial to note that these areas are not one and done though. Each must be constantly progressed and improved on as the change itself evolves.

RIPPLE AREA 1: YOUR CHANGE CORE

The first place to start is with the concepts we covered in Chapters 1 & 2 of this book. The three Valuable Questions:

1) Why are we doing this?

2) How will we prove it?

3) What are we doing?

Then using those questions as key building blocks, you create and strengthen your project spine.

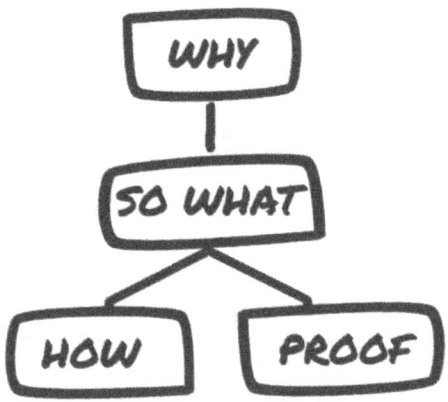

To be clear here, your 'How' can and should have inbuilt flexibility. But your WHY and Proof should be crystal clear.

Get this right, then move onto:

Ripple Area 2: Inside Your Change

There are three key elements to focus on here.

1) Elevating and maintaining team momentum and morale. Keeping your team(s) away from despair and shifting them from hopeful to fanatic.

2) Building and enhancing 'driver's aids' - those elements that make everyone's lives easier while driving regular upward improvement cycles. Use the Value Equation as a useful lens here.

3) Fostering a value-balanced Change Support Function to lubricate the gears and handle the friction between your change and your organisation's in-built bureaucracy.

Then, and only then, you can turn your eye to:

Ripple Area 3: Outside Your Change

There are again three areas of focus here.

1) Finding and enlisting the internal influencers that will make or break your change uptake.

2) Creating and growing peer-level sharing and adoption through effective community.

3) Strategic capability uplift of key stakeholders, leveraging natural human growth cycles.

Each ripple builds on the blocks before it. Do keep in mind here that each of the areas are not set and forget, rather they require ongoing refinement and attention to stay the course. This is not necessarily a sequential process, rather just an order of priority.

This brings me to the final note of this book.

Valuable Change is a Journey not a Destination

Argh, it's a horrible cliché. I almost feel dirty for using it, but frankly, it's a great metaphor for the imperfections of what we are aiming for here.

There is no perfect change.

Look under the cover of any change effort and you will see makeshift fixes, last minute scrambles and a few tactical untruths[61].

And that's OK!

It's the nature of life, the universe and everything.[62]

Valuable Change practitioners embrace the imperfection and move forward anyway. When you accept that there is no perfect strategy, technique, or delivery approach, you will suddenly find the one that works in your situation and use that one.

Perfection isn't the goal here.

Valuable Change is.

Good Luck.

---

[61] Not quite a lie, but not quite the truth either.
[62] Fun tidbit – this book is roughly 42,000 words long. For those of you who know the reference here, you'll also appreciate how great this coincidence is.

VALUABLE CHANGE

Chapter 9: TL;DR: Valuable Change In A Nutshell

At the start of this book, I mentioned that I would provide a summary chapter for those that are time poor, in need of a quick concept reminder, or just want the 'Cliffs Notes' version.

This is that chapter.

Drawing on the internet-concept of 'TL;DR', or 'Too Long; Didn't Read', (which really is the cheeky internet version of an executive summary), here is where I cram as many of the key concepts and takeaways from the previous 250 or so pages into just 10.

I'll echo my warning from the start of the book here though:

This Chapter DOES NOT hold the broader context and nuance that comes from reading the rest of this book.

Read it exclusively at YOUR OWN RISK.

About Valuable Change

Across the $10 Billion in projects that I've consulted on, only 15% have been able to succinctly answer three simple, but wholly fundamental questions:

1) What is the project doing?
2) Why are we doing it?
3) How will we know when we are successful?

So yes, that means 85% of these projects are venturing in the dark. Throwing money at an unknown result. This isn't just accepting ambiguity; this is driving off a cliff, blindfolded and hoping the car flies.

The good news is that you can have your cake and eat it.

There is a better way.

Your Change

A Valuable Change is one that solves a key organisational need or desire. It's truly as simple as that.

The trick is ensuring that your change actually solves that need or desire. This is where the art of asking the right questions becomes your key tool. A concise and considered answer to all three Valuable Questions is crucial for creating a great return on your project investment.

These 3 Questions are:

- Why Are We Doing This?
- How Will We Prove It?
- What Are We Doing?

Note: There is no need to require every project to have a financial return, as this is often just an exercise in mathematical theory (imaginary numbers!), with no relevance to real organisational return. This is a common trap that many organisations fall into.

Valuable Changes follow 2 key steps. These are:

- Step 1: Build The Core, and
- Step 2: Drive The Core.

STEP 1: BUILD THE CORE

In Step 1 you will Build the Core of your project, creating your project's spine. The Spine is a streamlined yet fortified backbone for your projects. It consists of only 4 parts: WHY, SO WHAT, HOW, and PROOF.

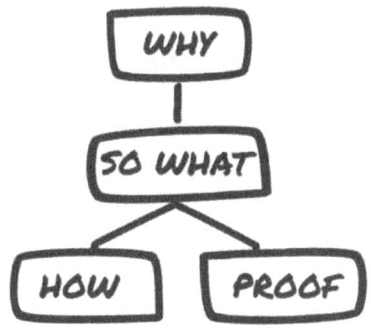

STEP 2: DRIVE THE CORE

Step 2 is to Drive the Core. You do this by building a fast, clear platform with as many driver's aids as possible. Driver's aids are those things that help your change efforts deliver faster, clearer, and more consistently. As a minimum you must:

- Embed your project's WHY and associated Proof Plan into your everyday decision making, and
- Ensure that your project is driven by its WHY not its' WHAT.

You also have other levers to pull to drive greater performance. These are your project's decisions, habits, and documentation.

YOUR PEOPLE

(Anecdotally), 95% of change initiatives require someone, somewhere to do something different. There's really only one true answer that consistently explains why someone does or doesn't do something, and that is the value of a reward compared to the pain required to receive it.

This is the **Value Equation.** Thankfully, the Value Equation is simple, and only has 3 parts.

1) The reward you receive for doing something.
2) The pain you must endure to get the reward.
3) The net result of the reward minus the pain, ultimately determining your decision to pursue the reward, or not.

You can think of it as an equation like the below:

$$\text{REWARD} - \text{PAIN} = \text{DECISION}$$

WIIFM (What's In It For Me) is the industry's go-to approach for driving change outcomes. But that's only half of the equation. **It doesn't matter what's in it for them if it's too painful to get!**

RALLY & CONNECT YOUR PEOPLE

You can't create change without your people. Accordingly, it's best to use an approach that focuses on everyone involved in the change. This means focusing on:

- Protecting your own team(s)' momentum, while
- Engaging and working with the right people across your organisation, and
- Maximising your change's organisational reach.

I recommend the Valuable People (VP) Approach, which has just 3 elements:

1. Build and Protect Core Momentum.
2. Identify and Enlist Internal Influencers.
3. Engage & Grow through Community.

Which, when put together, looks a little like the below:

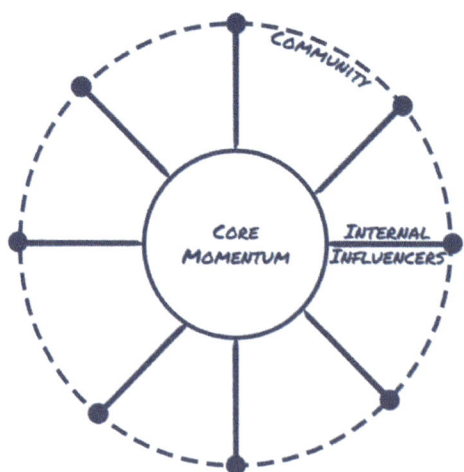

BUILD AND PROTECT CORE MOMENTUM

When considering momentum, you must look at two key elements – Hope and Energy. Energy is a sense of attentiveness, enthusiasm, and urgency. Hope can be thought of as a blend of the belief in the validity and usefulness of the work being done and an optimism for their personal future as part of this work.

The higher the energy and hope within your team, the higher the momentum. When plotted together we get the momentum path (shown below). The 5 levels, from Despair to Fanatic, cover the breadth of types that you will work with as you build momentum and morale within your change team(s).

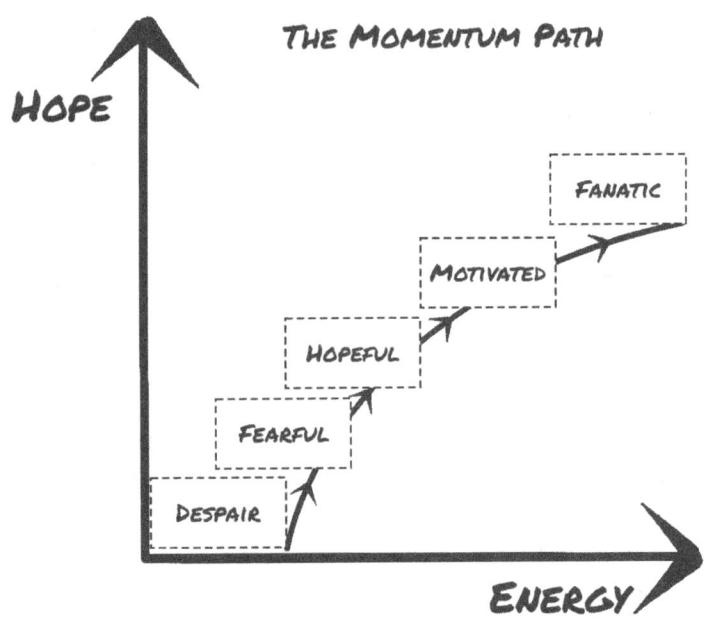

IDENTIFY AND ENLIST INTERNAL INFLUENCERS.

How do we best communicate, enlist and work with target groups of people across our organisations? Which, depending on the change initiative, can vary from 10 people to 10,000 people.

We find the people that connect the network together.

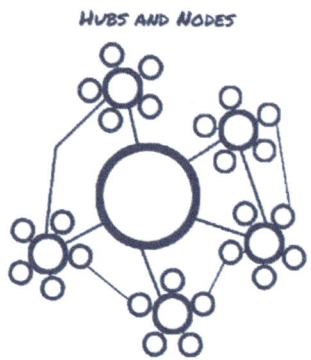

HUBS AND NODES

These people are your connective hubs, or more importantly for you, your Internal Influencers. These are the people to target and enlist as your change champions, and it's these people that we need on our side for maximum change adoption.

So how do we find your Internal Influencers? We ask their peers to identify them for you. For any group you are looking to identify the key internal influencers in, you merely need to run a survey that asks just 2 questions:

1) If you could work with any three people from across the <group/branch/organisation>, on any project, who would they be?

2) If you needed to be filled in on organisational news, key updates, or gossip, who would you go to first?

Then all you need to do is collate the data. A simple tally of the names is enough to get started. The more times a name comes up, the higher that person's internal influence.

ENGAGE & GROW THROUGH COMMUNITY

The final step of the VP model is to build a community around your change direction with your now secured influencers at the helm. The community forms a crucial role in our change efforts as it proactively provides peer-level support structures for your target stakeholders.

The key difference between communities that succeed and those that don't is the net balance of the Value Equation. There are 3 key avenues to boost the 'reward' column of your community's Value Equation:

1) **Exclusivity** – Your community can't be open to everyone.

2) **Reputation** – Your community must be held in high regard. Your community members must have a genuine advantage over those who aren't members.

3) **Edgy Content** – Don't be boring. Don't just say the same old tired things. If you have pursued both of the Exclusivity and Reputation avenues, then you will have a membership of high performers. Help them be even better.

Value Balance Your Change Support

Your change support function is often the conduit between your change efforts and your organisation's bureaucratic friction. So, it's worth getting right. But there's a major problem most organisations face here. Most change support functions fail. They become burdensome overheads. Unwieldy value-vacuums - sucking in time and effort from those around them and producing nothing worthwhile from it.

Thankfully not all Change Support Functions operate this way. The truly successful ones operate with a different mindset. **One of service**. The most effective Change Support Functions operate at the intersection of high trust and high value. This means operating within 'The High Value Service Cycle'.

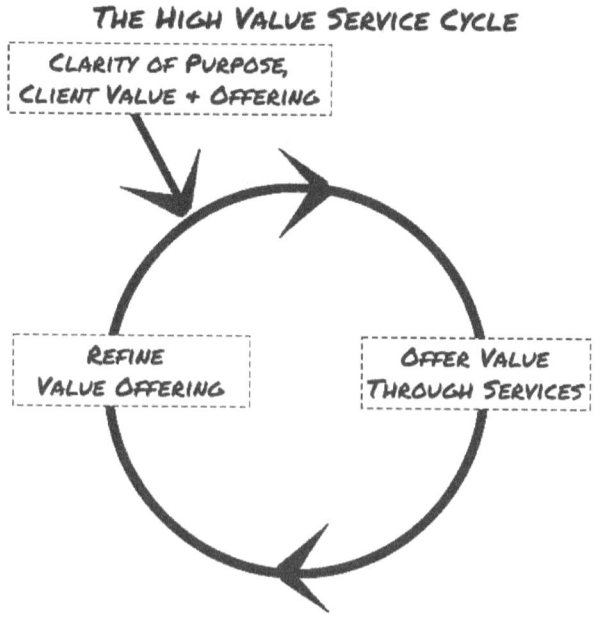

Your Next Move – Shift To Valuable Change

The great thing about the information, techniques and strategies in this book is that you can deploy any of them at any time in your change to enhance your results. While there is a loosely linear relationship between them, there are no hard dependencies from one to another. However, when prioritising where to start, you are best placed to think in terms of a 'ripple out effect'. Get the Change Core right. Then build Change Momentum within. Finally, solidify your Change Connections. These are not one and done areas, and must all be constantly progressed and improved on as the change itself evolves.

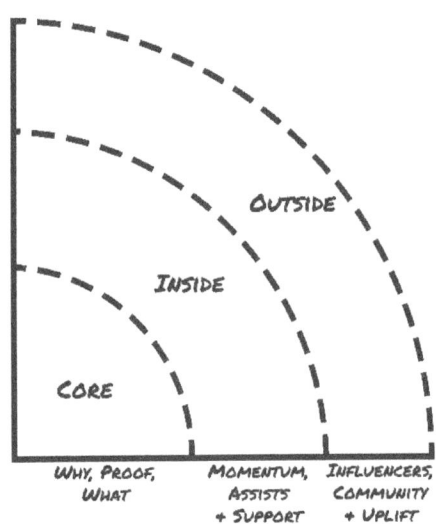

There is no such thing as a perfect change. Embrace the ambiguity, messiness, and imperfections. It comes with the territory.

ACKNOWEDGEMENTS

ACKNOWLEDGEMENTS

This book wouldn't have been possible without an untold number of people throughout my life. Life is the most wonderful adventure, and every moment and connection shapes who we are. So, with the admitted fallibility of attempting to acknowledge all those who had an impact on this endeavour, I'll try to keep this brief and to the point.

First and foremost, my wife, Naomi. The depth of our connection and mutual understanding was immediate from the very moment we met. No one knows me like you. Thank you for showing up each and every day and putting up with my endless discussions about this book. Including that time when you wanted to talk about the mysteries of the universe… and there I was sitting there pondering what size font to use.

Next, thank you to my girls, Adeline and Florence. Two bundles of endless energy. You keep me on my toes at all times, but your existence drives me to be perpetually better. I didn't truly know what aspiration meant until you came along.

Next, Dannielle and Ken. I couldn't even start to describe the endless ways that you have contributed to this book. Just know that I'm grateful for them.

Hayden, thank you for reminding me that all of the best books have dragons.

Brian, I'm always amazed at the uncanny amount of life coincidences we share. Life doesn't repeat, but it echoes, and we are living proof of that. Thank you proofing my books in absurdly quick turnaround times.

Valdi, my first work mentor and friend. Thank you for choosing the clown over the economist.

Andrew, thank you for plotting world domination via better consulting sales activity with me. Your deep well of candid kindness is much appreciated.

Carson, Steve, Chico and Jono. You all played a crucial role in this book. When I needed a mental break, you enabled it. ...Even if it was a romp around a Lovecraftian Europe in the early 20th century.

And finally, to all those that read this book. Thank you. A book without a reader is like a play without an audience - a mere echo. I sincerely hope this book helps you achieve your next change goal.

VALUABLE CHANGE

ABOUT THE AUTHOR: BRENDON BAKER

Brendon is converting others to a radical new idea… **Keep it simple.**

We are all involved in changing our organisations, whether we know it or not. The issue is the industry has over-complicated it. From the obtuse jargon and untold reams of paperwork. It's just too hard, too confusing, and too academic. You don't have time for that. No one does.

As a leading expert in the field, Brendon Baker has consulted on over $10 Billion in key transformation projects and programs across a range of industries. This has included public infrastructure, business/cultural transformations, shared service implementations, restructures, process overhauls, technology deployments, social policy & more.

Brendon Baker is the Managing Director of the Valuable Change Co.

His mission: Help Change Leaders Drive Real Value.

www.valuablechange.com

www.ingramcontent.com/pod-product-compliance
Lightning Source LLC
LaVergne TN
LVHW022002060526
838200LV00003B/66